BEER
GLORIOUS
BEER

BEER GLORIOUS BEER

Barrie Pepper and Roger Protz

Quiller Press

TESCO

This book is published with the generous support of Tesco Plc

First published 2000 by
Quiller Press Ltd, 46 Lillie Road, London, SW6 1TN

Copyright 2000 © The British Guild of Beer Writers

ISBN 1 899163 46 8

Designed by Jo Lee
Printed by Colorcraft Ltd, Hong Kong

No part of this publication may be reproduced in any way by any means without the prior written permission of the publishers.

CONTENTS

THE CONTRIBUTORS	vii
INTRODUCTION	
Roger Protz	xi
A HISTORY OF BREWING IN BRITAIN	
Richard Wilson	1
WHEN BRITISH BEER REALLY WAS BEST	
John Harrison	7
BREWING IN LONDON – The rise and fall of Southwark ale	
Helen Osborn	13
BURTON AS A BREWING CENTRE	
Christopher Marchbanks	17
EDINBURGH – Brewing capital of the Northern Hemisphere?	
Charles McMaster	23
TADCASTER – Burton of the North	
Barrie Pepper	27
PORTER AND STOUT	
Roger Protz	32
SHEPHERD NEAME – A story that's been brewing for three centuries	
Richard Harvey	36
STYLE OVER SUBSTANCE – The story of British Lager	
Jeff Evans	40
WELSH BEER – The unsung secret	
Brian Glover	45
SCOTLAND'S CASK ALE REVIVAL	
Allan Mclean	50
BEER AND BREWING IN IRELAND	
Carolynne Pepper	54
MANCHESTER ALE	
Graham Lees	60
MALT AND HOPS	
Keith Thomas	65
AN ECONOMIC SKETCH OF THE BREWING INDUSTRY	
Ivor Clissold	69

CONTENTS

THE FALL AND RISE OF THE MICRO-BREWERIES
    Alistair Hook   74

INDEPENDENT BREWERIES
    Michael Hardman   80

LOUIS PASTEUR AND THE BREWING INDUSTRY
    Nick Redman   85

BASS – A humorous view
    Maurice Lovett   90

THE BRITISH INFLUENCE – Today St Albans, tomorrow the world
    Michael Jackson   94

BRITISH BEER EXPORTS
    Mike Ripley   99

TRANSATLANTIC TASTE – one Yank's view of British beer
    Benjamin Myers   106

UK BEER EXCISE DUTY – A brief history
    Peter Ogie   110

BEER IN LITERATURE
    John Brice   115

THE BRITISH PUBLIC HOUSE
    Peter Haydon   122

PUB GAMES
    Arthur Taylor   127

BEER AND FOOD
    Susan Nowak   131

DIVIDED THEY FALL – A history of the trade associations
    Tim Hampson   135

MESSAGE IN A BOTTLE
    Richard Morrice   140

BEER IS BEST – the collective advertising of beer
    Fiona Wood   143

GENTLE GIANTS
    Roy Bailey   148

AND FINALLY...
    Barrie Pepper   153

INDEX
    Dave Hall   155

PICTURE ESSAYS
Pubs of the Cotswords and Thames Valley by Mark Turner   between 50-51
Inn Signs of England by Neil Holmes and Barry Pepper   between 50-51
A Pint of Beer by Steve Sharples   between 130-131

THE CONTRIBUTORS

Roy Bailey is a former film and television producer and cameraman who now makes cider commercially and writes about it regularly in CAMRA's *Cider Press*. He was a finalist in the BBC's *Mastermind* programme and also a specialist question setter in a later series on the subject of beer and brewing.

John Brice reports for several BBC radio programmes and was Highly Commended in the Guild awards for an audio history of CAMRA's first 25 years. He runs a brewpub in his home town of Chatham. He is a member of the Guild committee.

The late **Ivor Clissold** was a freelance writer and quality management consultant. He was beer columnist for the *Derby Evening Telegraph* and the author of *The CAMRA Guide to Cellarmanship*.

Jeff Evans edited eight editions of CAMRA's *Good Beer Guide* (1991-8). He contributes regularly to *Brewers' Guardian* and is a columnist for *What's Brewing*, specialising in bottled beers. His latest book, *The Good Bottled Beer Guide*, was Highly Commended in the 1998 British Guild of Beer Writers awards.

Brian Glover was Beer Writer of the Year in 1993 and twice winner of the Guild's silver tankard. He is the author of *New Beer Guide*, *Prince of Ales* and *World Encyclopedia of Beer*. He was editor of *What's Brewing* from 1978 to 1988.

Dave Hall is an indexer and proofreader specialising in beer, whisky, wine and food. He is a former licensee of a North Yorkshire pub that won several awards including Yorkshire Pub of the Year.

Tim Hampson is a freelance writer and was formerly Press Officer for the Brewers and Licensed Retailers Association. He has written and researched many articles on brewing and the brewing industry and the history of beer.

Michael Hardman has written many articles on beer, brewing and pubs for newspapers and magazines including the *Daily Mirror* and *Living in Surrey*. He is the public relations consultant to Young's brewery and produces and edits *The Ram Magazine*, which has won many prizes in the Communicators in Business Awards. Joint founder and first Chairman of CAMRA. He edited the *Good Beer Guide* 1974-77, and *What's Brewing* 1972-77. Author of *Beer Naturally*. He was the founder secretary of the Guild.

John Harrison is a retired materials scientist who presently acts as researcher for the Durden Park Beer Circle. He is a specialist in extracting brewing formulations from pre-1914 brewing books and ledgers and gylebooks and then making and enjoying the resulting ales and beers.

Richard Harvey is the public relations consultant to Shepherd Neame brewery, Kingfisher lagers, the Brewers and Licensed Retailers Association and the South Eastern Brewers and Licensed Retailers Association.

Peter Haydon is an author and freelance journalist and the general secretary of the Society of Independent Brewers. He wrote *The English Pub - A History* and edited *Which? Guide to Country Pubs*.

Alastair Hook is a brewer specialising in German brewing methods, beer styles and microbreweries. He is the brewer for Mash (London) and Mash and Air (Manchester). He is a former editor at large for *The Grist* magazine.

Michael Jackson is an author and broadcaster with many books and television programmes to his credit including *Beer, Michael Jackson's Beer Companion, The Great Beers of Belgium* and *The Beer Hunter*. He writes regularly for *The Independent*. He has twice been Beer Writer of the Year and twice runner-up and won the Budweiser Budvar travel busary in 1999.

Graham Lees is a widely travelled journalist having worked in Australia, Germany and Hong Kong. He was a founder member of CAMRA. His publications include *Good Beer Guide to Munich and Bavaria* and *The Encyclopaedia of World Beers*.

The late **Maurice Lovett**'s main interests in beer were the history of pubs and brewing but he also had more than a passing interest in the bizarre. He knew which licensee was known as Nocturnal Norman, who potted his false teeth on the pool table and where a pair of XXL ladies bloomers were found in the toilet cistern. For him therefore Bass in Art and Literature was a comparitively sensible subject.

Allan McLean collected beer labels in his native Edinburgh at the age of 12. William Younger's Pale Ale seduced his taste buds at 16. He learned more about ale in Yorkshire and his beer column in *The Scotsman* newspaper won him the Guild's Gold Tankard three times.

Charles McMaster was a co-founder and archivist of the Scottish Brewing Heritage. He is a freelance beer writer specialising in Scottish topics and a lecturer on Scottish brewing. His publications include *Alloa Ale* and *Chambers Scottish Drink Book*.

THE CONTRIBUTORS

Christopher Marchbanks is a journeyman brewer and brewing technologist who lives in Burton-upon-Trent. He is the author of technical brewing articles in *Brewing and Distilling International* and other brewing journals and of conference reports. He is presently a member of the committee of the Guild.

Richard Morrice is a keen supporter of independent brewers. He produces promotional material and runs consumer activity for all sectors of the licensed trade. Organiser of the Tesco Challenge.

Benjamin Myers writes about beer for a variety of magazines and newspapers, including the *Sunday Telegraph*. He received the Guild's Pewter Tankard in 1994 and the Interbrew Travel Bursary in 1995 and, in 1996, was named Beer Writer of the Year by the North American Guild of Beer Writers of which he was a co-founder. He currently lives in Los Angeles.

Susan Nowak was Chairman of the British Guild of Beer Writers from 1998 to 2000. She is a regular columnist for *What's Brewing* and her publications include *The Beer Cook Book* and five editions of *Good Pub Food*.

Peter Ogie is a professional brewer and former President of the Brewers' Guild and now retired after 35 years in the industry. An experienced consultant, judge and commentator whose contributions have appeared on radio and in the trade press. He is brewing correspondent of *Brewing & Distilling International* and writes regularly for *The Brewer*.

Helen Osborn is the Archivist for Young and Co's Brewery plc. She is a member of British Association for Local History and the author of *Inn & Around London: A History of Young's Pubs* and *Britain's Oldest Brewery: The Story of Young's*. Her main interests are the history of the public house and brewing history.

Barrie Pepper was Chairman of the Guild from 1991 to 1998. He writes for *What's Brewing, Pub Business, PubSpeak* and *American Brewer*. He has 14 books to his credit the most recent being *Irish Pubs, Fifty Great Pub Crawls* and *Walkers, Writers and Watering Holes*. He has been Highly Commended three times by the Guild in its Beer Writer of the Year awards and is the current Chairman of the Guild.

Carolynne Pepper specialises in research work and writing about women in the beer business. She has worked in beer sales for 11 years and is currently running her own speciality beer shop in Leeds.

Roger Protz was a founder member of the Guild. He is Editor of *The Good Beer Guide* and has written many other books with *The Taste of Beer* being his most recent. He writes for *What's Brewing, Licensee and Morning Advertiser, Guardian* and *The Observer*. He has twice been Beer Writer of the Year and four times runner-up in the Guild awards. He won the Budweiser Budvar travel bursary in 1996 and was Glenfiddich Drink Writer of the Year in 1997.

THE CONTRIBUTORS

Nicholas Redman is the company archivist of Whitbread plc. He is the author of *Whitbread in South Wales: A History* and *The History of Castle Eden Brewery*. He has been Highly Commended three times in the Beer Writer of the Year awards.

Mike Ripley was formerly Director of Public Relations for the Brewers and Licensed Retailers Association (formerly The Brewers' Society). In the 1980s he was closely involved in export drives to the USA and latterly to Japan. He is also a prize-winning author of thrillers.

Steve Sharples is a freelance photographer specialising in all aspects of beer and ales, their ingredients, brewing and the pub culture. Contributor to *What's Brewing*, *The Taste* and to national and regional newspapers and magazines. Publications include *Country Ales and Breweries*. He has exhibited at major UK galleries. Also specialises in commercial and jazz photography.

Arthur Taylor is the author of *The Guinness Book of Pub Games* for which he was Highly Commended by the Guild in its annual awards and *The Good Beer Guide to Northern France* for which he received the 1998 Budweiser Budvar travel bursary. He writes regularly for *What's Brewing*.

Keith Thomas is a technical writer for the trade and popular press, including *What's Brewing* and international publications and local newspapers. He is a specialist in brewing technology and co-ordinates training courses in brewing, dispense and flavour analysis.

Mark Turner is a freelance photographer and writer producing work for brewers, pub groups and various magazines. He contributes to the Anthony Blake Photo Library which specialises in pictures of food and drink subjects.

Richard Wilson was the author of *Greene King: A Business and Family History* and *The British Brewing Industry 1830-1980*. He has also written many articles on the brewing industry.

Fiona Wood is an economic brewing historian and former archivist for the Brewing and Licensed Retailers Association. She was the researcher for *The British Brewing Industry 1830-1980*.

INTRODUCTION

BY ROGER PROTZ

This book is a paradox. Why should the British need a book that extols the glories of beer? After all, despite the much-publicised problems of the brewing industry, with several closures among regional producers in recent years, Britain remains a major beer-drinking and producing country. Uniquely, it makes a substantial proportion of its beer in an unfinished form that reaches maturity not in brewery tanks but in casks in pub cellars.

The reason why we need such a book is locked in the curious refusal of the English (I absolve the Scots and the Welsh from the criticism) to acknowledge the things we do best. We disappear behind mounds of pasta and poppadums while English cooking withers on the vine. Rolls-Royce, Rover and other great car marques are flogged abroad. Even our language becomes more bastardised by the day as we are told to 'stand in line', avoid the risks of 'burglarization' (spelt with a 'zee'), and are urged to 'meet with' and 'talk with' people with David Frost-style mid-Atlantic accents who refer to 'President Bill Clinnun'.

I am not, Bacchus forbid, an English nationalist or xenophobe. A descendant of German immigrants to London in the mid-19th century, I am by nature and political outlook a passionate internationalist. But I am fascinated by the particular cultures and social mores of individual nations, and am baffled by English shoulder-shrugging at the very things that make this country both different and significant. We have, if we can hold on to it, a rich tradition of beer-making in Britain. The porters of the eighteenth century and the India Pale Ales of the nineteenth were pioneering styles that transformed

INTRODUCTION

both the manufacture and retailing of beer long before the lager revolution of central Europe. Britain's insulting interpretation of cold-fermented lager beers may now command around 50 per cent of total beer sales but it is a distress purchase snatched from supermarket shelves by people who pay more attention to saturation advertising than to aroma and flavour. (Jeff Evans' demolition of British lager is worth the price of this book alone.) In pubs, where we drink around seventy per cent of our beer, ale in all its forms remains the dominant beer style.

Yet who knows or proclaims this proud tradition? The posh prints have wine columns by the yard and only occasionally find time for beer. Jilly and Oz on Food and Drink ooh and aah like bibulous Bisto Kids over the juice of the grape but mention beer only when it's quirky, ale brewed by a vicar in his belfry and filtered through a choirboy's cassock. A writer rages in the pages of *Decanter* because the *Observer* gives more space to a column on pubs than to its resident wine expert. A *Sunday Times* writer sagely informs his readers that the British now drink more wine than beer, and we accept this as the given truth even though beer actually outsells wine by four to one. We assume, from ignorance and indifference, that beer is in terminal decline, consumed mainly by people who prefer a park bench to a conventional bed.

The problem is compounded by many brewers. As the late Maurice Lovett and John Brice show in their contributions, beer has featured powerfully in literature and art. Bass once bestrode the world like a brewing colossus. Its bottled ale and red triangle were celebrated wherever good beer was drunk and even stood proud on the bar of the Folies Bergere in Manet's noted painting. But today Bass has so traduced that heritage that it first dumps cask ales in favour of Caffrey's mock-Oirish nitrogenated 'smooth' beer along with sickly 'alcopops' aimed at the young and the gullible, and now is looking for an overseas buyer in order to leave brewing altogether. Whitbread, another world-famous name, is equally anxious to dump its history and its roots and become yet another pub group that buys other brewers' products. However much we may rage impotently when Bass and Whitbread are sold to the likes of Anheuser-Busch, Heineken, Interbrew or South African Breweries – companies with little understanding of the complexities and nuances of the British beer scene – it is the vendors who are most to blame. They will send a message to consumers that British beer is not important, that our proud brewing heritage is up for auction, not worth a mess of pottage.

In other words, we do need this book. We need it as a reminder of what British beer has achieved. Mike Ripley shows that it is still a force to be reckoned with abroad. Benjamin Myers and Michael Jackson underscore the importance of the British tradition to firing the enthusiasm of craft brewers and their mash tuns in other countries, most notably the United States. Allan McLean, Brian Glover, Graham Lees, Charles McMaster, Christopher Marchbanks, Helen Osborn and Barrie Pepper detail the vibrant contributions that Scotland, Wales and such brewing centres as Burton, London, Manchester and Tadcaster have made to British beer. And to prove that this is not an historical treatise, Alistair Hook, no mean brewer himself, shows that the small craft brewers in Britain, now numbering several hundred, have brought enthusiasm back to beer and have revived many lost styles.

Reading the book in manuscript form underscored for me the enormous contribution the British Guild of Beer Writers has made in its short life. As the founder member in the late 1980s, I was conscious that the Guild could not be the Campaign for Real Ale by another name. The suprisingly large number of writers who attended the first meeting I arranged in the Waterside Inn near King's Cross in London made it abundantly clear that even if I harboured such notions they had no intention of signing up to a body that would be CAMRA by the back door. The aims were different. We would leave it to CAMRA to lobby brewers, stage beer festivals, badger governments, and march in defence of threatened breweries. The Guild had a different job to do. It was enshrined in a mission statement that said: 'The Guild exists to improve the standards of writing and broadcasting on beer, the status of the journalists and authors involved, and the public's understanding and appreciation of the qualities of beer.' The Guild was scarcely up and running when Michael Jackson gave a memorable tutored beer tasting at the Lamb in Bloomsbury, attended among others by the respected wine writer Anthony Rose. The contributions in this book by Nick Redman and John Harrison recall the outstanding seminars the Guild hosted on the life and work of Louis Pasteur, and the impact and revival of India Pale Ale as a beer style. The book itself is being launched to coincide with a conference also called Beer, Glorious Beer in Burton-on-Trent to which editors and writers will be invited to hear the message that British beer is alive and kicking, and is as good if not a better companion on the dining table than wine.

Book and conference are timely. Beer writing has gone through a difficult period in the late 1990s and early twenty-first century. Not only does the media see wine as the fashion drink of the day but many editors in television and the press feel that in order to capture new readers among the young they must dump or sideline such 'old fashioned' drinks as beer. You sometimes wonder where such people go after work. A few days before writing this

INTRODUCTION

introduction, I did a beer tasting for a magazine in a bar in Islington devoted entirely to Belgian beer, more than two hundred of them. By nine in the evening the vast bar was engulfed by young people, handing over substantial amounts of money for some of the finest beers in the world: spiced white beers, Trappist ales, sour reds, fruit beers and lambics made by spontaneous fermentation. There was not a fizzy apology for lager to be seen. Here were several hundred young people drinking incredible beer but, according to the media pundits and the commissioning editors, they are the very people who do not want to read about that 'boring brown stuff'.

On the contrary, there is both a great thirst for knowledge about beer and a suprisingly high recognition rate among both young people in particular and all social classes in general. Near my home is a specialist Hogshead pub. It is close to several colleges and is popular with students. Ear-wigging in the bar (a favourite past-time of mine), I am delighted and impressed by the expertise of these young people. They call for cask ales, many brewed by obscure tiny craft breweries in isolated rural locations. Others choose Belgian beers from a cooled cabinet and I overhear conversations that indicate great knowledge of the subject and the subtle differences between a true Trappist ale and a commercial Abbey beer.

That knowledge comes courtesy of us beer writers. Our books really are read, despite what the royalty statements indicate. Sometimes articles from specialist publications seep into the broadsheets and from there even into the red-top tabloids. A few years ago the marketing director of Hall and Woodhouse in Dorset, which brews the Hofbrau beers of Munich under licence, told me the brewery had test-marketed a new lager in the homes of tabloid newspaper readers. He said he was astonished by the knowledge that many of them had about beer, in particular the 'battle of the Budweisers', the unending struggle between the American and Czech producers of the style. Again, that information came originally from the writings of specialist beer writers whose work has been picked up by the mass-circulation press.

There is no room for complacency. We need to redouble our efforts to win recognition for the singular contribution Britain has made to the world of beer. This book is a timely reminder of the importance of that contribution and how we must nurture it for future generations to enjoy.

I rest my case. More importantly, I rest my elbow on the bar and raise my glass to Beer, Glorious Beer.

Roger Protz, St Albans, March 2000

A HISTORY OF BREWING IN BRITAIN

BY RICHARD WILSON

'Beef and beer have made us what we are.'
The Prince Regent (George IV)

Although historically brewing is associated with Northern Europe, where the vine did not flourish, its origins are to be found in warmer climates. Reputedly, it was an article of every day consumption in Babylon in the fifth millennium before Christ. Certainly, it was brewed from barley by the ancient Egyptians and from there the art of brewing was transported to Greece. In 55 BC Julius Caesar found the Britons attached to malt liquor: they had 'vines, but use them only for arbours in their gardens. They drink a high and mighty liquor …made of barley and water.' Similarly, in the first century AD, Tacitus recorded that beer was the usual drink of the Germans.

The early supremacy of beer consumption continued across the first millennium AD, but details about its production in the so-called Dark Ages are lacking. Only when we come to the medieval period (1000–1500) do the main features of the trade emerge. Originally beer was domestically produced and a great deal of 'private' brewing remained for centuries (it was still around 50 per cent of total output in England in 1700), it began to be produced on a bigger scale in this period. Some of the larger monasteries and households of the nobility had facilities to produce hundreds of barrels in a brewing season; and everywhere beer was being sold retail from breweries and taverns.

BEER GLORIOUS BEER

On the demand side, the industry was sustained by a massive, if unquantifiable consumption. Amongst all classes beer drinking was heavy; wine and spirits consumption was confined to a tiny elite which in any case by no means despised beer and ale. Water, it seems, was taken only as an act of penance. Of course, not all beer was strong; a good deal of 'small' or 'table' beer – virtually non-alcoholic and brewed from the second or third mashings of malt – was drunk by servants, women and children.

Even in institutions like poor houses and schools beer was served to young and old alike. Indeed beer and bread were the common articles of everyday diet. Nothing was more deeply embedded in the culture of Britain than beer. It had the closest connections with farming; everyone knew how to brew beer. It was an integral part of all diets and medicinal practice; it was an essential aid to heavy labour; it was the corner stone of those celebrations so essential in the brief, hard lives of the vast majority of the population.

All beers were produced by a basic method. Malted barley, the manufacture of which was highly skilled in itself, was mixed with hot water to convert its starches into fermentable sugars. The resulting wort from which the spent grains had been removed (and subsequently used in livestock fattening) was then boiled with hops. Introduced into Britain in the early sixteenth century, these imported a delicacy of flavour and aroma as well as improving the keeping qualities of beer. After the hops were removed and the boiled wort cooled, yeast was added to achieve fermentation. Not until Pasteur's finding in the 1860s and Hansen's work on pure yeast in the 1880s, was its biochemistry understood. Previously fermentation was a hit and miss affair which troubled generations of brewers. After fermentation and cleansing the beer was drawn off for storage in vats or run straight into barrels. Here a secondary fermentation took place.

If brewing methods were unchanging, the variety of beers produced was nevertheless large. Each region had its specialisations. Some were famed nationally, like those of Burton and Dorchester; a few were traded, in small quantities, internationally. Transport costs, for a product which was too bulky and cheap to sustain high charges, and which in any case was not improved by transit, meant that the trade in beer – except by navigable water – was essentially local. Beer markets in the pre-railway age were, therefore, inevitably restricted. Only in the largest cities and ports did some breweries grow notably in size during the eighteenth century. This was most evident in London where the dozen great breweries producing porter achieved economies in scale because they possessed a big market on their doorstep. By 1800 the largest were producing 200,000 barrels a year. They had innovated in the use of steam power to facilitate bulk production. Moreover, a more consistent product was achieved by the introduction of the thermometer to measure temperatures accurately and the hydrometer to check specific gravities and determine the point at which to stop fermentation. Both were modest pieces of equipment but they led to important advances. These London porter breweries were one of the wonders of the first stages of industrialisation, essential attractions for every curious visitor to the metropolis.

From the nineteenth century a much firmer statistical base is available for the beer industry. It reveals high levels of consumption, peaking at an all time high of 40.5 gallons per capita for England and Wales in the late 1870s. Three central changes were taking place which transformed the traditional brewing industry in Britain. First, growth in consumption was fuelled (except in Ireland after 1850) by the general expansion of population and increase in living standards in the later nineteenth century. Much of the growth was concentrated in the rapidly expanding cities. Still involved in heavy manual work and now better off, the first two generations of Britain's industrialised, urban work force appear to have turned to an increased consumption of beer.

Secondly, there was a scientific breakthrough in beer production after 1875. Since Pasteur's and Hansen's researches were most applicable to lager brewing, they marked a parting of the ways in beer production. Both the bottom fermentation and decoction system of mashing (a more complex method in comparison with the infusion method of brewing described above) became prevalent in most European countries, the United States and, later, Australia. Essentially, these beers were all lager-type and depended for their brilliancy and quality upon bottom fermentation at low temperatures and maturation through a long, cool storage period. Lager had been known since the fifteenth century, but its production was limited until ice machines became common after the 1860s. Then the production of lager spread rapidly. In the United Kingdom, on the other hand, the production of lager-type beers never took off. Experiments in the 1880s and a very limited production thereafter were as far as the British went in this direction until the 1950s. Britain remained true to its top-fermented, cask-conditioned beer. Science in brewing was not ignored, especially in Burton-on-Trent and by Guinness in Dublin. Through better control of fermentation it allowed brewers to produce much more reliable beers which were, after the 1880s, lighter, less heavily hopped and more freshly brewed than the old strong ales which had been such a feature of the British beer market.

Lastly, the scale of production altered. The pace was neither rapid not universal. But the private and small producer was squeezed. Home production required space; it was a traditional rural occupation which could not flourish in the new cities. The small public house producer lacked the capital to realise the benefits of large scale production and to install the innovations of scientific brewing. Urbanisation and the railways opened up undreamed markets for commercial brewers on a scale which had hitherto only been realised by the great London porter brewers before 1830. Everywhere, as urban population burgeoned, the number of retail outlets grew rapidly. Most relied upon commercial brewers for their supplies because the advantages of small scale production was seriously undermined. These brewers completely dominated the market by 1900 (there were still around 2,000 firms) producing 95 per cent of output. Some were very large indeed; Guinness and Bass were the biggest in the world. But the scale of commercial brewing varied enormously. Guinness produced two-and-a-half million barrels by the 1900s. On the other hand there were scores of country breweries which survived to the First World War and beyond by brewing a few thousand barrels each year.

The Great War (1914-18) marked a watershed in beer consumption. Because supplies of barley and other brewing materials – sugar, maize and rice allowed into the mash tun after 1880 to produce lighter bottling beers – were severely controlled by governments anxious to protect food supplies and shipping prices rose sharply. Duties increased and production plummeted. And after 1920 the old pre-1914 levels of output were never achieved. The prime cause was not the depression which characterised so much of the inter-war period, although in its worst years (1920-23 and 1929-33) consumption levels were affected. Two other factors were probably more significant. First, the price of beer remained too high because of swingeing levels of duty, imposed during and after the Great War and again in 1931, came to form the major element in beer prices. For many people, high beer prices inevitably restrained consumption. Secondly, drinking habits were in themselves changing. After 1880 increases in the real wages of the working classes began to be expended on other leisure pursuits and other forms of consumer spending. Already per capita beer consumption was falling. The reasons were not the march of temperance, but new opportunities for sport and entertainment, and spending upon a whole range of cheap, mass-produced goods brought within working-class spending patterns for the first time. People began to live in more comfortable homes; they dressed better. Therefore the manufacturers of machine-made furniture, ready-made clothing and boots and shoes flourished. As a consequence spending in the old citadels of male working class life, the public house, showed their first signs of decline.

After 1918 this process speeded up quite rapidly. Those in work increasingly preferred to spend their incomes on leisure alternatives. The range of these was extended dramatically by the cinema, the radio and, for some, the motor cycle and the motor car. Although the retail outlets for beer were improved to cater for new consumer preferences, they began to lose their old central role in working-class existence. Moreover, the nature of beer itself changed to reflect these shifts in consumer demand. The high pre-1914 gravities never returned. Generally, beer was much weaker. Bottled beer made great strides. It was more convenient; it was lighter in flavour and more easily stored; it could be drunk at home. Its popularity reflected the profound changes taking place in social habits.

Again, the brewing industry was badly disrupted by the Second World War (1939–45), and restrictions after this meant that normality in the industry was slow to resume. Gravities again drifted lower after 1940. Then, from the late 1950s consumption rose sharply following half a century of contraction. Once more the dramatic turn around in the industry reflected profound shifts in the social habits, preferences and tastes of post-1960 society. On the supply side the surge in demand for beer appears to have been sustained by the prosperous 18–35 age group. They preferred lighter, lager-type beers which were increasingly retailed in supermarkets, although there was a renaissance in those public houses providing food and entertainment. The beer market was transformed by these trends. Lager formed well under five per cent of beer consumed in the early 1950s; by 1990 it accounted for more than half of all beer brewed. Beers were increasingly packaged in cans and bottles. And with rising incomes and an increasing propensity for travel the beer trade became more internationalised as the interests of the biggest firms crossed national frontiers. As a consequence of these changes production soared up to 1980, since when it has stagnated and declined in the 1990s. Yet even at its height in the 1970s per capita consumption did not approach late-nineteenth-century levels: beer consumption at its 1979 peak was only two-thirds of its late 1870s level. And of course beer on average in the late 1970s was considerably weaker than a century earlier – 3.8% abv as against approximately 5.7% abv. Moreover, the industry developed alcohol-free beers (not exceeding 0.05% abv) and low-alcohol beers

(0.05%–1.2% abv) in the 1970s and 1980s. Technically it was difficult to brew tasty versions of them. Both were aimed at the responsible drinker when driving, both were expensive to brew and to market.

Production has also changed, in scale as well as technique. There has been, since the late 1950s, a notable contraction of brewing firms and as modernisation and rationalisation proceeded rapidly throughout the brewing industry since the 1960s consumers interest in every aspect of beer and its history has surged in the last 25 years. It has sought to protect the great traditions and variety of the remarkable industry whose roots are so deeply embedded in British culture.

WHEN BRITISH BEER REALLY WAS BEST

BY JOHN HARRISON

There was a time when British beer, for range and quality, was regarded as the best in the world. Unfortunately for present day beer lovers this time occurred more than 120 years ago, between about 1860 to 1880. British brewing rose from mediocrity in 1650 to its peak between 1860 and 1880 and has slowly declined thereafter. In 1650 British brewers had just about come to terms with what continental brewers had discovered some centuries earlier, that the hop was the best herb for flavouring and preserving beer. The best of the unhopped ales, such as Mumm and Welsh Ale, were putting up a strong rearguard action but hopped beer was king.

The range of beers made in 1650 was very limited. Few breweries made more than three ales or beers. They were all nut-brown to brown in colour and usually consisted of a strong ale, ale, and table ale or table beer. (See Appendix p.12 for the meaning of the term ale after the disappearance of unhopped ale.) Many small breweries made only one grade of beer. Hop usage was low – nine to twelve ounces per barrel. In a nutshell, British brewing in 1650 was undistinguished.

The first of many developments that were to upgrade British brewing occurred around then. A group of Derbyshire maltsters found that whereas coal was a poor fuel for the curing of malted barley, coal that had been preheated to drive off all the volatiles – coke – was an excellent fuel. It imparted no foreign flavours to the malt and the heat was readily controlled by using dampers on the air supply. These two advantages enabled maltsters to produce pale malt, and thus pale ales, for the first time.

The production of pale malt was a major innovation. It not only led to the introduction of a completely new range of pale ales but also indirectly to a new attitude to the use of hops in beer. This came about that when using the old-style nut-brown and brown malts, brewers had experienced no problems in fermenting the nut-brown ales during the hot summer months of May to September. So it came as a shock to find that fermenting pale ale worts at much above 70°F resulted in serious off-flavours including high ester contents and excessive acetic acid. It is not known who introduced the notion of making March and October beers. However their introduction enabled pale ale brewers to cease production in the summer and maintain supply from heavily hopped beers made between February and April and matured in cellars until needed. A good example of the practise is given in the brewing books from the Truman brewery for 1832.[1] In the winter their XX ale at an OG of 82 used 4 ½ lb of hops to a quarter of malt. The last batch before ceasing production (7th May) used 8lb of hops to a quarter of malt, but the March beer (for drinking in late August to September) used 12lb of hops to a quarter of malt. October ales were different. They were made in October with new malt and new hops at OG's 100 to110, well hopped, and were kept one to two years as a reserve stock. Handfuls of hops were pushed into the barrels before bunging and thus the practise of dry-hopping was originated.

Thus in the space of a few decades, a new range of pale ales was introduced and a new philosophy regarding the use of heavy hop additions to keeping beers. The last major innovation before 1750 was the introduction of porter in 1722. I have never believed the accepted story that porter was just a brewery ready-mixed version of something that could be produced in a tavern by part-filling a tankard from three separate barrels. Porter took off like a rocket. Virtually all London brewers were porter-brewers by 1726 and the style spread rapidly into the provinces. The explanation offered by Corran[2] seems much more plausible. This suggests that porter was developed by a London brown ale brewer to compete more effectively with incoming pale ales from outside London. London well water was too high in bicarbonate to make good pale ale but was quite satisfactory for dark beers. Quite apart from porter being a good beer, Mathias[3] identified several factors that gave porter an economic edge over pale ales of the same OG. Satisfactory porter could be made with second quality grain and old hops, whereas good pale ale needed the best pale malt and good quality hops. Porter could be brewed all year round and its resistance to the effect of high temperatures during fermentation enabled it to be fermented in very large vats. Lastly the maturation of porter in bulk meant that barrels were only needed to convey beer from the brewery to the customer, thus reducing considerably the stock of barrels needed. The porter style eventually found its way to the Empire, Russia, the Baltic States and Eastern Europe.

The first important advance in the period 1750 to 1850 was the use by Richardson (1777–85) of the hydrometer to show that the extract from brown malt was 12 to15 per cent deficient compared with pale malt.[4] This discovery led to a rapid change in the formulation of porters to a typical equal quantity mixture of pale malt, amber malt and brown malt. Meanwhile, in a small brewery at Bow in Middlesex, George Hodgson was experimenting with pale ale for the India trade. By 1800 he had settled the formulation and mastered the techniques of production, storage and packaging, and was virtually a monopoly supplier to the East India Company. This monopoly was only broken when Burton pale ale brewers looked for new markets to replace their lost Baltic trade. Their India Pale Ale replaced Hodgson's India Ale by 1835.

Meanwhile the development of the drum grain roaster by Wheeler[5] in 1817 was causing yet another change in porter formulations. The drum roaster enabled malt or raw barley to be roasted to a brown-black colour and then quenched with a waterspray to prevent a runaway conversion to charcoal. Black malt and roast barley had high colouring power and the reformulated porters used pale malt to provide most of the fermentables; amber or brown malts for flavour; and small amounts of black malt or roast barley for colour and flavour. These new porter formulations were very flexible and played a major role in the expansion of porter from a two-beer family in 1800 (porter and common porter) to the 6 to 8 beer family of porters and stouts by 1850 (see graph overleaf).

Another input into the porter scene was the decision by Arthur Guinness and Co. in 1827 to enter the English market with its Extra Superior Porter of OG 73. The formulation of Irish porters was different to that used in England. The grist consisted of 95 per cent pale amber malt plus 5 per cent roast barley.[6] The output from the Dublin brewery, much of which eventually came to England, rose from 45,000 barrels in 1830 to one million barrels in 1880.

The period following 1830 was a golden one for British brewing. Apart from a small tiff in the Crimea there were no major wars; Britain was the workshop of the world and the rapid rise in population, particularly in towns, provided a steadily growing market for its brewers; the licensing laws and excise duty were not onerous; and the expanding Empire

A TYPICAL LONDON PORTER BREWERY

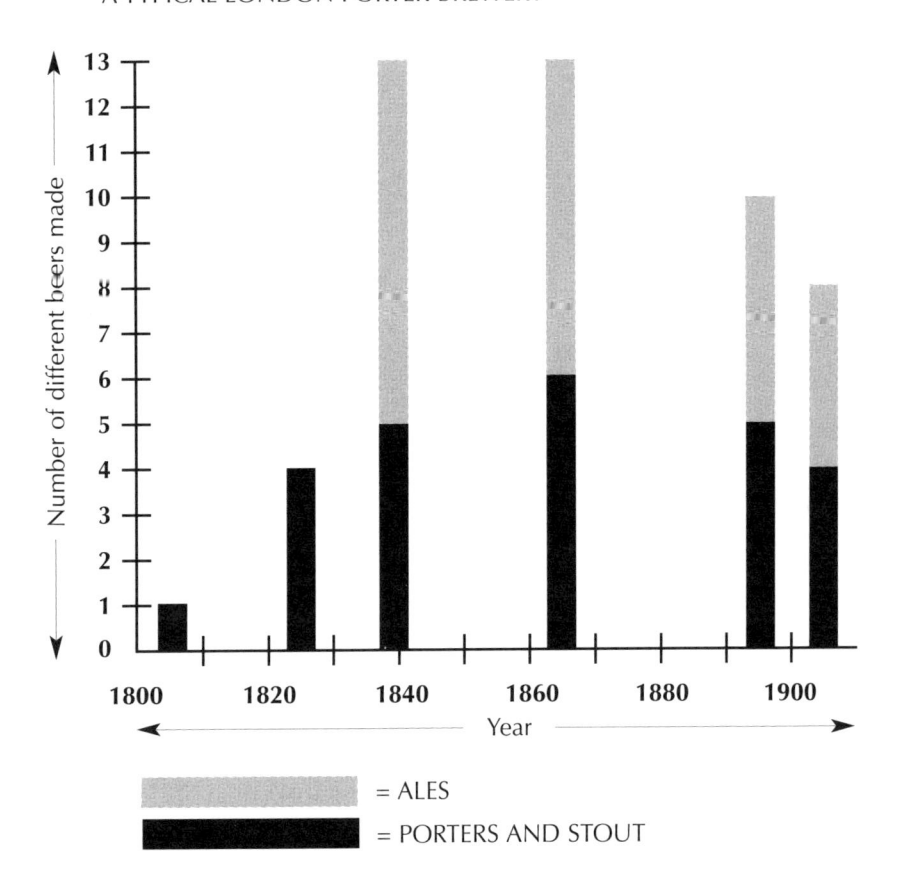

Bar chart: Number of different beers made vs Year (1800–1900), showing Ales (grey) and Porters and Stout (black).

- 1800: 1 (porter/stout)
- 1820: 4 (porter/stout)
- 1840: 5 porter/stout, 13 total
- 1860: 6 porter/stout, 13 total
- 1890s: 5 porter/stout, 10 total
- 1900: 4 porter/stout, 8 total

= ALES
= PORTERS AND STOUT

increased the prospects for overseas sales.

1850 to 1880 were the golden years of British brewing. By 1850 brewing was becoming a mature technology. The two main areas of weakness being a lack of understanding of the biochemistry of malting, mashing and fermentation and a lack of ability to control temperature during fermentation. Some small brewers with ample access to deep well water had been using cooling coils fed with well water at about 50 F since the early 1800s, but this facility was not generally available. It was not until Harrison of Australia developed mechanical refrigeration in 1857 that temperature control became a practical possibility for the large scale brewery. His refrigerator used diethyl ether as the working fluid, other working fluids tried included CO_2, SO_2 and methyl chloride. However these were largely superseded when Linde developed the ammonia system in 1873.

With a maturing technology, and large expanding markets, brewing flourished as never before. The range of beers made by large breweries in the peak period from 1860 to 1880 would put most existing breweries to shame. In the mid1870's, William Younger of Edinburgh on two sites produced 26 different beers. The beer menu read as follows: Scotch Ales 1, 2 and 3; Scotch Ales (London) 1, 2 and 3; Ale No 4; Ale No.3 Pale: 160 shilling Ale and 140/-, 120/-, 100/-, 80/-, 60/-, 50/- Ales, X Ale, XX Ale, XXX Ale; X Pale, XX pale; Stouts 1, 2 and 3; Double Brown Stout; XXXS Strong Pale Ale; Majority Ale and table beer. The OGs ranged from 35 to 137. The changing range of beers offered by a typical London porter brewery is shown in Figure1, the peak occurring about 1855-60.

A second marker for the peak in British brewing is the extent to which adjuncts or extenders are used in the grist. Up to about 1880 in England and 1900 in Scotland beers were made using all-malt grists. From about 1880 onwards rice, flour, maize meal and brewing sugars became an increasing percentage of the grist. The only exceptions were export beers which retained the all-malt grist.

Over the past 25 years but more intensively the last 15 years, the Durden Park Beer Circle has been researching, making and evaluating pre-1914 beers. Almost without exception the beers from the golden age are superb. To come across one such beer in an evening's drinking would be an event to remember. They were of course high gravity beers compared with those produced today. Regular porters, pale ales and bitters had OGs of about 60, stouts were about 70, double stouts 85, triple and export stouts 95 to 107. In the X ale range single X was about 55 to 60, XX 70, XXX 85 to 90 and XXXX 95 to 110.

There was no single over-riding cause for the decline of British brewing. The temperance movement played a part as it became more influential through the nineteenth century. The movement contained two strands; the religious strand advocated total abstinence from alcohol on ethical grounds, whereas the industrial strand, which recognised the dangers posed by having alcohol-affected workers in steel mills, coal mines and heavy industry in general, advocated responsible consumption of alcoholic beverages.[7]

In 1880, Gladstone withdrew the malt tax and replaced it by a tax based on the OG of the wort before fermentation. This had two undesirable effects. Stronger beers paid more tax, and because strong beers usually need longer maturation compared with lower gravity beers, the tax had to be funded for a longer period before the return came in from the beer sales. Once established, the beer tax became an easy source of revenue. For example the tax on a 36-gallon barrel of standard beer (OG 57) in 1880 was 6s 3d. In 1914 it was 7s 9d, 50/- in 1918 and 100/- in 1920. Beer gravities also took a dive during the first world war, reaching 40 in 1918 and 31 by 1919.

There is no doubt that British brewing went through a golden age in the period from 1860 to 1880. It is equally certain that the tax regime and the drink-drive laws will not permit mass-drinking of regular beers at an OG of 60 plus. However there is no reason to think that those magnificent beers could not make a come-back as beers for special occasions. If and when they do, a bit of the golden age could well return.

Appendix
With the demise of unhopped ale between 1650 and 1700 the term ale lost its original meaning. It was adopted by hopped beer brewers with different meanings in different parts of the country. In London around 1850, if you wanted porter you asked for beer, if you asked for ale you got pale ale. In the south west the term beer was reserved for strong old ale. In the Manchester area, ale (particularly strong ale) was called beer and porter was called porter. In the north east, the term ale was used to describe a drink made with malt and treacle.[6] Currently it means a top-fermented beer in the British style.

References
1- London Record Office – *Truman's Brewing Book 1832*
2- Corran HS – *A History of Brewing* – London 1975
3- Mathias P – *The Brewing Industry in England 1700-1832*
4- Richardson J – *Statistical Estimates 1784*
5- Wheeler D – *British Patent 4112* 1817
6- Tizard WL – *Theory and Practise of Brewing* – London 1857
7- Monkton H A.- *A History of English Ale and Beer* – London 1966

BREWING IN LONDON
The rise and fall of Southwark ale

BY HELEN OSBORN

And if the words get muddled in my tale,
Just put it down to too much Southwark ale

So says the miller from Chaucer's *Canterbury Tales*, written in 1387. Brewing was the major industry in Southwark for over 500 years and Southwark ale was famous the length and breadth of the country. Common Brewers were established in Southwark as early as 1336. London in the 14th century was tiny in comparison with the capital today, yet it was by far the largest city in England. The populated area consisted of the City within the old Roman walls, Westminster, and Southwark, connected by London Bridge, the only bridge over the Thames. Southwark not only housed the brewers, but also the foreigners, the brothels, the theatres and bear pits and some of the capital's finest galleried inns. It was an exciting and energetic place to be. In choosing the banks of the Thames at Southwark, those early brewers were putting brewing right at the heart of London and it is not surprising that their ales were famous. The Thames provided transport potential, the capital provided a captive market, high quality malt was not far away in Hertfordshire, and wells sunk deep into the artesian basin provided plentiful, good quality brewing water. It is a mistake to suppose that London brewers have ever brewed with Thames water, since its main use by Londoners has always been as a vast open drain.

Chaucer's ale was brewed without hops in the traditional medieval English manner, but Southwark was one of the first places in the country that brewing with hops caught on. Hops were introduced in about 1420 from the Low Countries. By 1440, new 'beer' brewhouses were established in Southwark that were large enough to employ several labourers and sell beer in bulk to publicans rather than selling everything retail as was the more common practice. The threat of the new fangled beer was considered so great that the Brewers Company was granted its Royal Charter in 1437 in order to fight for the traditional unhopped English ale. But the new beer had the great advantage of keeping better. It could therefore be distributed further and produced in greater quantities. The tide of innovation could not be turned and brewing with hops was to spread from London throughout the country. Thus in Southwark a change was set in motion that resulted in the most important revolution in British brewing.

Closely following on the heels of the beer brewers, came the hop merchants who also chose to make Southwark the centre of their operations. Again, this was no accident since the Old Kent Road leads straight into Southwark from the hopfields of East Kent. Other hop markets existed, but Southwark always had the wealthiest merchants and hop factors. As transport improved in the eighteenth and nineteenth centuries, even Burton turned more and more to Southwark for its hops.

When Stowe, the London historian, was writing his *Survey of London* in 1598 there was already a flourishing export trade in goods from London using the Thames. Southwark beer was used not only to provision ships, but also to sell abroad. Those sixteenth century breweries clustered along the river in Southwark and to the north near the Tower of London and in this small area, there were 26 Common Brewers and 15 breweries were worthy of note by Stowe. The Thames foreshore would have been festooned with sails and rigging and loud with the sound of casks being loaded from the brewers' wharfs on and off ships.

The beer brewer in London wasn't doing anything that couldn't be repeated in any country brewhouse with good water and malt, the difference was merely one of scale until the eighteenth century and the birth of porter. From the 1720s to the 1830s porter was the dominant beer style in England and was first and mainly brewed in London where the water was suitable. Most authorities agree it was a thick, dark, bitter beer of some strength. The much repeated story is that it was first brewed in 1722 by London brewer Ralph Harwood, but in truth its origins remain obscure. It is very doubtful that the appearance of porter owes everything to one brewer as the innovation was as much one of malting as of brewing as it would have needed a more highly dried malt to produce a blacker beer.

At first, porter could not be made fine or bright and so was matured for a few months in cask before being sent out. From the 1740s isinglass was used to help clear the beer of sediment, but by then the advantage to the brewers of maturing porter for a year or more in vat was becoming obvious. Both these developments helped to make porter clear, but it still could not become bright and this made it greatly suited to London water. Larger amounts of porter could be stored and for longer than other beers, larger amounts could therefore be distributed and at far great distances. In consequence, London brewers, who already had a head start on the rest of the country, started to become truely rich and were able to move up in society. The writer Smollett declared, 'The only genuine and wholesome beverage in England is London porter'.

Larger and larger vessels were built to store porter and there was quite a competition in London to build the biggest tun. Visitors to the London breweries always marvelled over the size of the tuns and some of the biggest were christened by holding parties for 200 people inside them. This crazy spiral of one-upmanship was bought to an end in 1814 when a 20,000 barrel whopper owned by Meux and Co burst open, releasing a flood of porter and drowning some hapless passers-by.

The survival of of the names of so many of those porter brewing families is testament to the fame of their products. Only they rose to massive production in the eighteenth century and they established the structure of the industry in London for the next 200 years. The few who stuck to brewing 'ale' produced no more than 30,000 barrels a year, whilst the porter breweries reached 300,000 by the end of the eighteenth century and Trumans rose to 500,000 by the mid-nineteenth century. Among the well known names were Whitbread, Courage, Calverts, Reid and Co, Hoare and Co, and Barclay Perkins. Dr Johnson remarked whilst helping to sell Calverts Anchor Brewery to Barclays, 'We are not here to sell a parcel of boilers and vats but the potentiality of growing rich beyond the dreams of avarice.'

But public taste can be fickle and the nineteenth century public were wooed away from the dark bitter stuff to the bright sparkling ales of Burton on Trent. Once Burton was connected to the capital by train, the beer practically poured down the track, pushing porter to one side. The repeal of the duty on glass in 1845 also helped Burton as drinkers changed from their pewter mugs to glass which showed off a bright sparkling ale to great advantge. The London porter brewers were slow to switch to ale production and the Burton brewers seized the initiative by buying pubs and depots in London from under their noses. By the end of the nineteenth century most of the big London brewers had built separate ale houses alongside their older porter breweries. Production was kept separate in order to treat the 'ale' water with gypsum to 'Burtonize' it. From then on it was downhill all the way for porter and production slowly dwindled until finally halted by the second World War.

If late eighteenth century porter was the zenith of London's brewing expertise, then the nadir must be the period known as the 'merger mania' of the 1950s and 60s. Watneys of the Stag Brewery, Pimlico, relative newcomers to brewing, who had already merged with Coombe and Reid and Co, pioneered keg beer in the 1930s and started to market it aggressively in the 1950s. The rest, as they say, is history. This was one innovation that the general public did not care for, but by the time CAMRA became a force to reckon with, the damage in London was done. The sole remaining brewer of the eighteenth century who maintains a presence in Central London is Whitbread – but not to brew. Their porter Tun Room where visitors once marvelled at the huge vats and the quantity of beer they enclosed, is now hired out for functions and the brewery buildings house only a corporate headquarters.

London has never seen such a dearth of brewing activity. The massive porter breweries are gone or metamorphosed into something else and the brewers have turned their backs on Southwark and Central London. Southwark ale has vanished. Two small South West London outposts, Youngs of Wandsworth and Fullers of Chiswick, now carry the flag for brewing in London. The irony is that before the middle of the nineteenth century they would not have been considered London brewers at all, Wandsworth and Chiswick were still part of the countryside. Yet they are all that remains of the hundreds of breweries in London and its environs from the earliest days.

BURTON AS A BREWING CENTRE

BY CHRISTOPHER MARCHBANKS

E ntering Burton upon Trent from the north by its newest bridge over the railway (built in 1993) there is a skyline of chimneys, kilns and long large buildings that herald an intense monoculture of brewing. Step outside and the smell confirms the industry of Burton.

This short review of the development of Burton upon Trent as a brewing centre over the past 300 years shows four distinct periods which have overlain the continuous production of high quality beers.

Like most small towns it emerged after the dissolution of its Abbey in 1540 as a village with a population of 1,000 carrying on normal agricultural and related milling and cloth activities. Brewing, throughout the country at that time was a small cottage industry, but Burton already had a good reputation based on the Abbey brewhouse.

In 1699 the unique brewing story begins to unfold. The Trent Navigation Act put Burton at the head of the river's navigation system which was completed in 1720 with wharves at the western end of the town. The main commodities traded were pots, coal, cheese, millstones and ale outward with a return load of timber, iron goods, corn and chemicals. The ale would be the nut brown strong beers from Burton which were known in London as excellent, if expensive Burton or Darbie Ale.

The population was now 2,000 and the town had two common brewers, the name given to brewers who sold to the free trade, plus 30 to 40 licensed victuallers (brewpubs). The brewing equipment was simple and portable, a combination of wooden vessels, boiling coppers with wooden and metal implements. These would be housed in a relatively small building. Close to the brewhouse may have been a maltings which needed more floor area and specialised kilns to cure the green malt.

The businesses would be small and similar to today's microbrewers making up to 15 barrels per day (3,000 barrels per annum). The maltster would make two tonnes of malt per day (400 tonnes pa). Both businesses would employ two or three people including the owner for about 30 weeks a year, as production would only be carried out in the cold months of October to April each year.

Such a scene introduces the first period – 1740 to 1815.

During this period we find the juxtaposition of

> a) Large quantities of potable water, initially taken from shallow wells near the river. As larger volumes were required new deep wells of over 1,000 ft, known for their high gypsum content, were sunk to the north of the river.
> b) Improved navigation as the Trent and Mersey canal was completed in 1770, linking the two rivers to Hull, Liverpool and Bristol.
> c) Entrepreneurial flair and capital from local landlords and merchants. They expanded brewhouse output by supplying strong Burton beer for home and export markets. The export trade was very cost effective as the Burton beer to the Baltic countries went as 'ballast' for ships bringing timber, iron, flax, hemp and grain to England.

These first brewing companies, occupied premises north of the river, very few of their buildings remain today but some names live on including Clay, Salt, Evans, Wilson, Bass, Sketchley and Worthington. The Baltic trade was run by these merchant/owners who often had interests in both the outward (beer) and inward cargoes. It was never very large – the best year was 1775 when 11,000 barrels went to Russia. By 1801 it was down to 8,000 barrels from a town with a population of 6,000 and then 17 common brewers. In 1801 the estimated total output of Burton was 25,000 barrels. per annum. The beer exports ended abruptly in 1807 when the Napoleonic blockade cut off the route from Hull to Russia – the blockade continued until 1815 by which time the trade had gone and the brewers of Burton had reorganised through bankruptcy and amalgamations.

Which led to the second period – 1820 to 1840.

By 1822 the consolidation had reduced the number of common brewers to 5, with increased output. Increased output was achieved using new technology and economies of scale. Agencies were set up in all major cities where bottling from hogsheads was carried out. In addition a new initiative was undertaken to develop a Pale Ale for export to India (IPA) in competition with the India Ale brewed by Hodgson in Bow, London. The new beer was pale, bitter, sparkling and able to withstand the long hot sea journey. It was first accomplished in 1822 by Samuel Allsopp (who married into the Wilson family brewery and changed the company name). He used only the finest barley malt, hops and brewing water from the deep wells which was sulphate rich. It was an instant success and provoked many imitators.

By 1841 Burton had a population of 8,100 and the output had increased to 70,000 barrels. from 11 brewing companies which now included several newcomers including J Marston in 1835 and J Thompson in 1840.

Distribution was greatly extended and speeded up when the Birmingham to Derby railway opened in Burton in 1839 with branch lines into many of the town breweries. The export market for IPA was not very large – a maximum of 15,000 barrels but its quality and reputation was the springboard for a world wide expansion of Burton's fame for luxury, clear, sparkling pale ale in bottle as well as cask.

Coupled to this fame was the development and expansion of Burton upon Trent into one of the wonders of the Victorian era. The fruits of scientific research, higher wages and better living standards resulted in an enormous building programme in Burton particularly by Bass and Allsopp to meet increased national beer consumption.

This ushered in a long sustained third period – 1845 to 1900. The established companies built new large brick maltings and breweries near to the railway and incorporated steam powered equipment to improve efficiency. Larger batches and refrigeration allowed malting and brewing all year round.

New companies were established to supply malt (Meakin, Cherry and Yeomans), brewing plant (Briggs, Morton, Thornewill), casks, wood turning, yeast and processing by products such as yeast extracts (Marmite). The legacy of that vast building programme punctuates the skyline today with some fine solid buildings.

In 1859 Bass and Allsopp set up their own internal railways linking the main line with their many warehouses, criss-crossing tracks over the town road with 24 steam engines and related trucks. They were finally phased out in the 1960s.

This expansion required greater understanding of the brewing process to ensure beer consistency. Scientific innovation and research was first introduced into brewing in Burton (and the world) by Allsopp in 1845 with the appointment of Mr H Bottinger as chemist. Soon after other eminent scientists joined Bass, Worthington and Salt doing research into beer, the microbiology of beer spoilage and starch chemistry. For their contributions to science some were honoured with prizes and election to Fellowship of The Royal Society. Their early scientific meeting group – The Bacterium Club which started in 1876 was the predecessor of today's Institute of Brewing. One notable development is the Burton Union system for fermentation. Recent investigation has unearthed a patent granted in 1838 to Peter Walker – a brewer of Liverpool for an 'apparatus to be used for cleansing beer' which describes a Union system. This was most likely first tried out in Liverpool as Walker did not build a brewery in Burton until 1877. Nonetheless the system was a success and it was noted in Bass in the early 1840's. Most Burton breweries installed the Union system during the boom period of 1855-1890. Less successful was the short-lived lager brewing venture by Allsopp in 1899 when they built a lager plant in Burton.

During this period the Burton population grew enormously. From 1851 it increased by 10,000 every 10 years so that by 1900 the population was 50,000. The number of breweries peaked in 1888 at 31, declining to 24 by 1900 when the estimated annual output was 3,500,000 barrels. The large London brewers with their falling Porter sales looked enviously at Burton and either built or bought breweries in town so as to compete.

The new entrants included: Ind Coope (1856), Charrington (1872), Truman (1873), Mann, Crossman & Paulin (1874) plus others from Lancashire (Walkers, Boddington) and Leicester (Everards).

By 1890 the peak was over, to be followed by another industry contraction. This was caused by a combination of high cost public houses (the Burton brewers had hitherto relied on free trade so had left pub purchases too late), fierce price discounting, the temperance movement, recession, war and the general improvement in beer quality from all breweries throughout the country.

So started the turbulent fourth period from 1914 to the present day.

The Burton trade was static if not in decline, which was a reflection of the national situation. Beer sales continued to drop between the wars because of recession, public house legislation, high beer duty, improved homes and living standards, better roadways and alternative leisure activities (such as sport, the cinema and travel by public transport and private car).

The consolidation was first at the local level (1920-35) and then at a national level (1955-65). Burton suffered in the first period as the London brewers withdrew and local brewers amalgamated so by 1939 only 6 breweries remained in Burton producing an estimated 2,000,000 barrels.

By the mid 1960's the decline of bottle and cask beers had stopped. Cans and filtered draught beers were increasing and distribution was switched from rail to motorways. This gave the two largest Burton brewers, Bass and Ind Coope (the latter having merged with Allsopp in 1934) renewed activity. The brewing of lager beer was also re-introduced to Burton with new National brands.

By 1970 nationwide amalgamations had formed six national brewery companies producing 80% of the UK output from 30 brewing units spread over the UK. Two of the largest units and the two largest national brewers were based in Burton Bass and Allied Breweries (successor to Ind Coope).

New large maltings (50,000 tonnes pa) and brewery modernisations (up to 2,500,000 barrels pa) were required to take advantage of automation and computer technology. It changed the skyline again as concrete tower maltings, skin clad brewhouses and outdoor rocket shaped fermentation tanks were built.

The brewing infrastructure in Burton also altered with the demise of wooden casks and the mechanisation of maltings away from the town. Their place was taken by metal cask, label, beer mat, and amusement machine manufacturers. The brewery plant and process engineers remained with new modern products for world brewing markets.

Rationalisation continues as the century turns with Carlsberg – Tetley (successor to Allied Breweries) selling its Burton Brewery to Bass in 1998 who combined it with its existing brewery to make it 'Britain's Biggest Brewery' with a brewing output of more than 5.5 million barrels per year.

With the population static at 55,000 the output from the town's four brewhouses in 1999 is possibly at its highest ever (more then 4,000,000 barrels), producing an even greater mix of beers.

There is a high percentage of lager beers now brewed in Burton, some made under license or contract from global brewers, plus the world famous Burton Ales and Pale Ales from Bass. Pedigree Bitter from the only brewery in the world still using the Burton Union System is brewed by Marston Thompson and Evershed. They were taken over in 1999 by Wolverhampton & Dudley Breweries with the pledge to keep its pedigree secure. To complete and renew the cycle new generation microbreweries have returned. The Burton Bridge Brewery opened in 1981 – currently has three pubs in the town and also sells its prize winning draught beer to the free trade away from Burton together with its bespoke hand bottled beers.

Long may the cycle turn as new micros are drawn to expand the reputation and produce world famous beers from Burton upon Trent – the centre of brewing.

EDINBURGH
Brewing capital of the Northern Hemisphere?

BY CHARLES M^CMASTER

Edinburgh can rightly lay claim to being one of the foremost brewing centres in the world. Until very recent years the brewing industry dominated Edinburgh, as did no other single industry, by its very presence, being everywhere apparent right across the city from Craigmillar to Shandon. Described by no less a person than the famous nineteenth century writer and journalist Alfred Barnard as 'Burton and London rolled into one' as far as breweries were concerned, it remains even today a brewing centre of some significance and is the headquarters of Scottish Courage, one of Britain's largest brewing and leisure groups.

Brewing in Edinburgh has a very long history dating back at least to the twelfth century when the monks of Holyrood Abbey took advantage of the pure water, good barley and plentiful fuel in the vicinity to commence the brewing of ale. This met with sufficient success for the brewing tradition to become, within a couple of centuries, a widespread domestic activity, seasonal in nature and closely connected to the agrarian cycle.

Much domestic brewing was practised in the home by women who would only produce sufficient for the needs of themselves and their immediate families, but commercial brewing-for-sale came early to Edinburgh and by 1598 a powerful Society of Brewers was established to control and regulate all aspects of the trade, from the sinking of wells, the purchase and malting of barley and the supply of coal. They were granted monopoly privilege within the Burgh and outside competition was expressly debarred. Over the following centuries commercial brewing gradually overtook domestic brewing and by the mid-eighteenth century began to predominate with the appearance of what were to become some of the most famous names in Scottish brewing history – Archibald Campbell in 1710, William Younger in 1749 and Andrew Drybrough in 1750, to name but a few. By the mid-nineteenth century Edinburgh could boast some forty breweries in all and was acknowledged as one of the foremost brewing centres in the world with Edinburgh Ale sold simply as such and exported worldwide.

In particular the Edinburgh breweries were concentrated in the Canongate (the lower end of the Royal Mile), the Cowgate, the Pleasance and the Grassmarket areas, for it was here that an underground trough of water-bearing strata, which ringed the city, existed and was known familiarly as the 'Charmed Circle'. As the nineteenth century unfolded numerous breweries were established on the eastern and western outskirts of the city at Craigmillar and Gorgie respectively, but still tapping into the same water-bearing strata. Although by this time Edinburgh had been a brewing centre of importance for centuries its highpoint came towards the end of the Victorian era and coincided with the height of British imperial expansion. Edinburgh's success as a brewing centre of world repute was largely based on the brewing of Pale Ales, which came much into vogue by the mid-nineteenth century, replacing the older, dark Scotch Ales and Porters. Edinburgh's hard water was particularly suitable for the brewing of these types of beers which travelled well on long voyages overseas, kept their condition in hot climates and, as a result, were ideally suited for the export markets. Indeed, special Export, Imperial and India Pale Ales were brewed for these markets and the latter in particular (IPA) became something of an Edinburgh speciality.

Many famous names came to be associated with brewing in Edinburgh: Aitchison, Bernard, Campbell, Deuchar, Drybrough, Jeffrey, McEwan, Mackay, Morison, Murray, Younger and Usher, among others, but two companies in particular, by their very size and presence, dominated the brewing industry in Edinburgh by the end of the nineteenth century. These two were Wm. Younger and Co. Ltd., and Wm. McEwan and Co. Ltd., the giants of the Edinburgh brewing scene.

The first William Younger established what was to become a brewing dynasty in nearby Leith, the port for Edinburgh, in 1749, and towards the end of the century moved into the city itself. Unrelated to any of the other brewing dynasties in Scotland the firm that was to become Wm. Younger and Co. Ltd. was to grow to the extent that by the late nineteenth century it was operating no less than three large breweries in the Canongate area of

Edinburgh and could boast of a trade which reached to the furthest outposts of the British Empire.

The only other brewing company in Edinburgh which could compete with Younger's in size and influence was that of Wm. McEwan and Co. Ltd. William McEwan hailed from Scotland's other famous brewing town of Alloa and did not establish his Edinburgh brewery until 1856, yet within a few decades, through hard work and business acumen, he had built his business into one of the largest brewing concerns not only in Scotland but anywhere in Britain. William McEwan took particular advantage of a relatively new mode of transport, the railway, which he had laid right into his brewery. This helped the rapid growth of his company. McEwan secured large military contracts and this ensured that his beer was widely exported as well as being very popular on the domestic market.

From about 1880 the number of breweries in Edinburgh gradually began to decline as the trend towards larger units coupled with the capital costs of embracing new technology, such as refrigeration and gas and electric power, inevitably led towards amalgamation and rationalisation. This was compounded by the effects of the First World War with its raw material, output and gravity restrictions and the disruption of sea-borne commerce. These factors, combined with a prolonged inter-war depression, particularly on the domestic market which saw sales fall to less than half of the pre-war total, drove some companies out of business and left the remainder both with little money to reinvest and dependent to a disproportionate amount on their export markets. The two great Edinburgh rivals, Younger's and McEwan's, came together in 1931 to form Scottish Brewers Ltd. in particular to more efficiently exploit their overseas trades.

The Second World War and its aftermath brought about a new set of problems for the Edinburgh brewers, of which there were still nearly twenty. Britain's diminishing world and colonial role and the independence movement badly hit the export markets and in an attempt to secure a share of a flat domestic market brewers embarked upon a tied-house buying spree, the main result of which was to get many heavily into debt. In addition, brewers everywhere were burdened by historically high levels of excise duty. As a result, by the mid-1960s, there was substantial overcapacity in the brewing industry in Edinburgh and self-regulatory moves towards further rationalisation came to naught, leaving individual companies vulnerable to takeover from outside interests.

The early 1960s were the locust years of the brewing industry in Edinburgh. Brewing groups from England (Vaux, Watney, Whitbread) and from overseas (Carling) gained control of a large part of Edinburgh's brewing industry and many famous names began to disappear. From some sixteen breweries in Edinburgh in 1960 the number was reduced in a decade to seven and this decline continued through the 1970s and 1980s until today there remain only two breweries in Edinburgh, Fountain and Caledonian (plus a handful of pub and micro breweries) although the city remains the headquarters of Scottish Courage. Perhaps the most significant event of recent years, and one which sums up the recent concentration of Edinburgh's brewing industry, has been the closure in 1986 of the historic Holyrood Brewery, last of Edinburgh's Canongate and Old Town Breweries. With its closure brewing was brought to an end on this site for the first time in some eight hundred years.

TADCASTER
Burton of the North

BY BARRIE PEPPER

The Romans called the town Calcaria because of the abundance of fine magnesian limestone there and which, ten centuries on, was used to build York Minster. And although brewing was known to take place in the town during the fourteenth century it was not until the eighteenth that full advantage was taken of the special properties of the local well water and commercial brewing began in earnest.

The town's history starts with the Brigantes and it has been occupied successively by the Romans, Danes, Saxons and Normans. Saxon King Harold moved his troops from Tadcaster in September, 1066 to defeat the invader Hardrada of Norway at Stamford Bridge. Days later after a 250 mile trek south he was to die in defending his country against William of Normandy at the Battle of Hastings. Later Tadcaster became a thriving coaching town which at its height serviced more than 50 stage and mail coaches each day.

The first record of brewing in Tadcaster was noted in 1341 and although there is no record of a brewer in the town in the 1379 poll tax returns this may be because brewers were often shown as innkeepers although in nearby Wetherby the return showed three brewers there.

In 1758 John Hartley, the town's postmaster and David Backhouse, landlord of the White Horse, opened a brewery behind the inn in the High Street. It was the forerunner of the present Samuel Smith brewery and remains as the oldest one operating in Yorkshire. Hartley's family ran the Royal Mail operation in Tadcaster as well as the brewery through four generations and whilst it ran profitably when coaching and posting flourished the coming of the railway led to fewer inns and less demand for their beer.

By 1847 the brewery was run down and it was then that John Smith, a tanner from Meanwood in Leeds, bought it from Jane Hartley a surviving widow of the postmaster's family. He had two brothers: William who entered the business with John as a partner, and Samuel who remained in the family tanning business in Leeds. Both John and William were bachelors.

The business did well initially under the Smiths but on John's death in 1879 it was once more moving into deterioration. The remaining brothers were not good friends and John's will did not help matters. The brewery building was left to them both in common for their lives but after that it reverted to the sons of Samuel being the only male heirs in the family. The business was left jointly to the brothers and William bought out Samuel's share. Samuel died in 1880 and his brother refused to take his son, also called Samuel, as a partner when he came of age in 1882.

Young Samuel was left with a derelict brewery and William proceeded to build a new brewery almost next door at a cost of £130,000. He took with him the business and the trade names and it opened in 1884. Two nephews, sons of his sister, joined him in the venture and, at his request, added the name Smith after their existing name of Riley. Riley-Smiths were directors of the company for many years and it is a name that exists to this day in the town.

When William died in 1886 the nephews had a thriving business. In six years they saw its barrelage rise from 25,000 to 150,000 a year. In 1892 the company was incorporated but the Riley-Smith brothers maintained control. Henry Riley-Smith was the first chairman and remained in the position for twenty years.

Meanwhile the young Samuel Smith refurbished the old brewery and in 1886 started brewing again. At the same time a new brewery had been built on the western side of the town on land bought from the North Eastern Railway. It was a redundant plot left over from an abortive attempt in 1845 by George Hudson, the 'Railway King' to link York with Leeds. All that remained of his labours was several acres of land and a handsome viaduct across the River Wharfe which stands today and is still known as 'Hudson's Folly'.

The new brewery was built by Hotham and Company which was based in York. The move to Tadcaster was made for two reasons: the York brewery was too small to cope with an increasing trade, and the standard of water in there produced poor quality beer. Tadcaster was an obvious place to move to. Not only was there plenty of room to build and to expand but it had good rail and road communications. Twenty years after Hudson's attempt a new railway line opened between York and Leeds and the road system was already well established. And, of course, there was the water.

No time was wasted in building the new brewery. The land was bought in February, 1882 and by November of that year an advertisement in the *Yorkshire Gazette* stated that the company was now in business at Tadcaster and had changed its name to The Tadcaster Tower Brewery Company. It seems likely that brewing started there in February, 1883. The partners of the company in those early days were all nobility including the Earl of Durham and his three brothers, baronets, a son of a Viscount and the brother of a Marquis. Not without reason was it known as the 'Snobs' Brewery'.

By 1886 Tadcaster had three large breweries all operative and serving areas well beyond the pale of the town. It took its place behind London and Burton but alongside Edinburgh, Dublin, Alton and Wrexham amongst the important brewing towns of Britain. Contemporary accounts show that the three largest common brewers, John Smith, Samuel Smith and Tadcaster Tower were all producing excellent quality ales.

There were also two smaller breweries: the Victoria Brewery in Chapel Street and the New Brewery both acquired in 1895 by Braimes Tadcaster Breweries Ltd. In 1903 this company amalgamated with Leeds City Breweries Ltd and the Tadcaster plants were closed down.

It was the start of a period of expansion particularly for John Smith's. Before the turn of the century the firm had acquired brewing businesses in Easingwold, Sheffield, Bridlington, Thirsk and Great Driffield. Some were taken over simply for their tied estates and the breweries closed but others continued brewing for many years. By 1901 ordinary shareholders were receiving a 27% dividend. In the new century many more acquisitions followed. Metcalfe of Pateley Bridge, Cockayne of Sheffield, Fernandes of Wakefield and Warwicks of Boroughbridge were among them. All had a substantial number of outlets and this built up the estate to more than 700 properties. By the second world war John Smith's was one of the country's major brewers.

Samuel Smith's brewery has a far less exciting history although this may well be because of the reticence of the company to say much about itself. Its own 200 word history says more about its namesake rival than itself. Samuel Smith continued in charge at the brewery until his death in 1927. His son Geoffrey then carried on through his lifetime and in 1964 his two sons Humphrey and Oliver took over and remain there. It is the quintessential family firm and one of the few regional brewers in Britain not to have a Stock Exchange listing.

The firm acquired two small breweries in the 1940s: McQuat of Leeds with its nine pubs in 1947 and the Rochdale and Manor Brewery in the following year. Brewing ceased immediately at McQuat's but continued in Rochdale until 1974. Before the purchase of the two breweries 62 per cent of sales went to the free trade much of which was to clubs in the West Riding of Yorkshire.

'Sams' has remained a firmly traditional brewery using the Yorkshire square method of fermentation to produce its cask beers. Only five other breweries use this system which claims to produce full, smooth beers. The firm also uses wooden casks for all its cask conditioned beers and has one of the few cooper's shops in the brewing industry as well as a team of dray horses which are still used for local deliveries.

Tadcaster Tower brewery was not very acquisitive although its predecessor, Hotham and Company, had picked up a goodly number of pubs in York. The Victoria Brewery at Burton Salmon with its 13 pubs was bought in 1896 and the following year 21 pubs were leased in Durham followed by 20 more in 1903. The estate consisted of 160 freehold pubs and 190 leaseholds. New depots were opened and steam wagons were brought into use for deliveries.

Between the wars only one substantial purchase was made, that of Cattle's of Pocklington. The ten pubs were kept but the brewery and plant were sold. In 1921 the lease of all the original property in York – the offices and about 50 pubs – was purchased for £40,000. The final link with Hotham was broken. And in 1930 Hinde's of Darlington with seven pubs was bought for £35,000 to become the company's north-eastern depot to serve a growing estate in Durham.

The Samuel Smith company has remained independent from its incorporation but the other two Tadcaster breweries both fell to take-overs in the post war period. The Tower Brewery was bought by Hammond's of Bradford a firm badly in need of expansion and a better image. It was said in the West Riding that there were three types of beer: good beer, bad beer and Hammond's. Tadcaster provided both expansion and quality. The Bradford brewery closed in 1955 and the company went through a series of take-overs and mergers until today Tadcaster Tower forms part of the giant Bass plc. Its modern plant produces mainly keg beers for national distribution.

John Smith's continued on its acquisitive path. Between 1958 and 1962 it took over Whitworth of Wath upon Dearne, Yates of Manchester, the Barnsley Brewery Co and Warwicks and Richardson of Newark. Between them they owned more than 500 licensed premises. Both the Whitworth and Yates breweries closed on purchase but the other two continued brewing for some years. But by 1970 although it ranked high amongst the nation's brewing companies with more than 1,800 houses and 700 employees, it was acquired by Courage, Barclay and Simonds of London.

The moves that followed did the company's brewing reputation no favours. In 1972 Courage became part of the Imperial Group and the mighty corporate hand not only closed down the much loved Barnsley Brewery with its assertive ales but stopped the brewing of cask conditioned beers at Tadcaster for seven years. Then the Hanson Trust bought out Imperial but it had no feel for brewing and sold off Courage to the Australian predator Elders IXL.

Courage opted out of pub owning after the government reaction to the Monopolies and Mergers Committee report by swopping its pubs for Grand Met's breweries. Then in 1995 the group was bought once again, this time by Scottish and Newcastle and the brewing arm languishes under the strange name of Scottish Courage. But at Tadcaster the trading name of John Smith remains and Yorkshire beers are still brewed from local water.

PORTER AND STOUT

BY ROGER PROTZ

Porter is an enigma. Its origins are obscure, shrouded in mystery and legend. Yet it remains a potent link between modern ale brewing and its medieval past, using at first the ancient method of 'staling' beer in wooden vessels and then, with the new technologies of the industrial revolution, dark roasted malts, storage in cooled underground tanks, steam engines, mechanical pumps, and powered rakes for stirring the mash.

Too many people who tackle the history of porter ignore its social roots. It coincided with the painful and protracted changes in England that turned a feudal agrarian nation into the world's first fully-fledged capitalist market economy. In the process, tens of thousands of impoverished rural people poured into towns and cities to work in factories and mills. In a brief moment of history, London was turned from a sprawl of loosely connected villages into the greatest city in the world. The new urban proletariat had to be housed and fed. Beer brewed in pubs could not meet the insatiable demand for ale that not only refreshed the urban poor but briefly ameliorated the squalor of their lives in London's burgeoning slums. Commercial brewers rose to meet the demand, which, from the early 18th century, was for a dark beer that became known as porter.

According to legend, the first porter (or 'entire butt beer' as it was then called) was brewed in 1722 by a brewer called Ralph Harwood in his Bell Brewhouse in Shoreditch, in London's East End. It was called 'entire' because it attempted to replicate the flavours of three different types of beers that were combined together. Legends die hard. While Harwood undoubtedly brewed an ale that became the talk of London, spawned countless imitations, and encouraged to likes of Samuel Whitbread to concentrate solely on porter brewing, Harwood was not the first producer of porter. Rather, the origins of combining three types of beers to create a porter beer occurred earlier outside London and, as is so often the case where beer is concerned, are connected to taxation. In those days, tax or duty was paid not on the alcoholic strength of beer but on its ingredients, malt and hops. Coal was also heavily taxed while wood was not. So while the technology existed to produce pale malt cured over coal or coke kilns, most brewers stayed loyal to brown malt cured over untaxed wood fires. The cost of making beer was exacerbated by Britain's long-running wars with France. To help the war effort, the British government loaded tax on malt, hops and coal.

The result was that pale beer brewed outside London – where coal fires were banned as a result of fumes and fogs caused by the fuel – became expensive due to the high cost of coal and was drunk mainly by the better-off from specialist retailers known as 'ale drapers'. It was known as 'twopenny ale' as it cost twice as much as brown beer. 'Stale' also came from country brewers, who bought fresh brown ale from London pub-brewers, stored it in oak tuns for up to a year and then sold it back to the London brewers for twice the price. This mature beer was known as stale as a result of attack by wild yeast strains in the unlined tuns that gave it a lactic, sour character. (The famous 'red beer' from Rodenbach in Belgium is still made in this fashion and the Rodenbach family is thought to have learned the technique from English porter brewers; Guinness Foreign Extra Stout, brewed in Dublin, is still a blend of fresh and staled stouts.) As the tax on malt was higher than the tax on hops, London brewers developed a new type of well-hopped beer made from brown malt. But at a time when most beer was stored or aged for several months, the new brown beer was too young and harsh for many drinkers' tastes. Thus started a craze in London for mixing or blending beers in order to create the flavours demanded. The result was 'three threads', a blend of three beers: pale, stale, and brown. The name came from the fact that the beers were taken from three separate casks in pub cellars, into which pouring taps or spigots were threaded. Three threads, while not called porter at the time, is the origin of the porter style.

Ralph Harwood's 'entire butt' beer was an attempt to meet the large consumer demand with a single beer that replicated the flavours of three threads, allied to a desire to cut out the country brewers and maximize his own profits. Some brewing historians have suggested that Harwood brewed two or three ales, blended them and served them from one butt or cask. It is unlikely that he had sufficient space in his small pub-cum-brewery or the necessary equipment to make several ales. What is more credible is that he brewed a single beer but inoculated it with a small amount of stale bought from the country brewers to give it the lactic tang enjoyed by drinkers. That is certainly the technique that was used by the great porter brewers, including Arthur Guinness in Dublin.

So while there is little doubt that the first entire butt was brewed by Harwood, the roots of the porter style lie in the three threads established earlier, which is what Harwood's entire butt tried to replicate. We will never know what Harwood's entire butt beer tasted like because we have no idea what ingredients he used, though there is speculation that he may have bought an improved type of brown malt from maltsters in Hertfordshire. One thing is certain: the success of his entire butt sent his trade of publican-brewer into terminal decline. The demand for entire was so great that Sam Whitbread moved from a small ale brewery not far from Shoreditch into new premises in the heart of the City of London where he brewed only porter and its stronger version, stout porter. By the late 18th century, Whitbread's brewery was one of the wonders of the civilized world with steam engines, a Porter Tun Room 'the unsupported roof span of which is exceeded in its majestic size only by that of Westminster Hall,' and a series of underground cisterns, each one holding the equivalent of 4,000 barrels of beer stored and cooled by pipes through which cold water was pumped.

By the turn of the 19th century Whitbread was brewing 122,000 barrels of porter and stout a year. The commercial porter brewers were part of the powerhouse of the new economic order. Within a century, brewing had changed out of all recognition. One of the many reasons why we shall never know what the early porters tasted like is that they varied so much from brewery to brewery and even from pub to pub. Entire butt beer was not even precisely the same as porter, though both styles tended to be known by the generic term of porter as a result of their popularity with the vast army of market porters working in London streets. An 18th-century print from the Whitbread archive shows a pub advertising on its fascia 'Whitbread's Entire and Porter'. Whitbread, as the archive indicates, produced both styles.

Porter and entire were brewed primarily from brown malts: it was not until the tax was lifted on coal and coke that brewers, with the aid of saccharometers, could see the greater sugar extract available from pale malt. The use of brown malt then went into decline. For the first century of their production, entires and porters were brown rather than black beers. The switch to pale malt meant that brewers had to colour their beers to give them the aspect demanded by entire and porter drinkers. The invention in 1817 by Daniel Wheeler of a malt roasting cylinder, similar to a coffee roaster, enabled brewers to use chocolate and black malts for the first time. Jet-black porters and stouts were the result. There are many superb revivalist porters and stouts being brewed in Britain today. They are all based on mid to late 18th-century recipes. Those first entires and porters, which spawned not just a beer style but the world's first great commercial brewing industry, remain tantalizingly out of reach.

SHEPHERD NEAME
A story that's been brewing for three centuries

BY RICHARD HARVEY

Shepherd Neame's brewery in Faversham has been brewing beer without a break since 1698 – longer than any other brewery in Britain. Set in the heart of Kent's hop country, Shepherd Neame is the last surviving brewer of any significance in the county and has become, therefore, the sole guardian of Kent's unparalleled brewing tradition.

Cluniac monks were brewing ale in Faversham 500 years before Shepherd Neame was founded. When King Stephen built an abbey in 1147, it didn't take the Benedictines long to discover that the town's water combined with locally-grown malting barley produced an exceptionally fine ale.

So, when a mayor of the town, Richard Marsh, opened his Faversham Brewery in Court Street (known then as North Street) in the late seventeenth century, its future success was assured. The brewery is still set over the same 200-feet-deep artesian well which supplies some of the purest brewing 'liquor' in the region.

The minutes of the Faversham Wardmote at the beginning of the eighteenth century reveal that Marsh was the largest of 23 brewers in the town. But just a few years later the number of other brewers had dwindled to five.

The Faversham Brewery remained in the hands of the Marsh family until 1741 when the ownership passed to Samuel Shepherd and thereafter by direct descent through four generations to his great-grandson Henry Shepherd. In 1817, with Julius Shepherd at the helm, the weekly wage bill had escalated to £8.4s.6d!

In 1864, when Percy Beale Neame joined the firm as a partner, it became known as Shepherd Neame and Co. The brewery became a limited company in 1914, since when a succession of Neame family members and their relatives has presided in the boardroom. Today the chairman is Robert (Bobby) Harry Beale Neame, great-grandson of Percy, and his great-great-grandson, Jonathan, is managing director.

During the early years of the Faversham Brewery its catchment area was very much determined by the limits of the horse-drawn drays, which was probably ten miles at most. But in 1857 records show that beer was shipped from Faversham Quay by sea nearly 20 miles to Sheerness on the Isle of Sheppey where the Fountain Hotel supplied local customers.

When the London Chatham and Dover Railway arrived in Faversham in 1858 the brewery was quick to break free of its confined trading area by opening a network of rail-side stores. In 1871 a store at Camberwell gave the company its first foothold in the London area.

This expansion was strengthened by setting up agencies throughout the south-east and by 1878 these were servicing nine areas as far apart as Woolwich, Sevenoaks, Hastings and Folkestone.

During this period of unprecedented expansion it was decided that it would be most economical to deliver beer to the stores using the brewery's own rail trucks. By 1874 there were ten of them, each capable of carrying 60 kilderkins to the stores where the barrels were loaded onto one of the brewery's fleet of 44 horse-drawn drays.

Always a company quick to keep ahead of progress, Shep's bought two steam traction engines in 1887. Contemporary correspondence reveals: 'We have two: one six-horse, the other eight-horse and what we chiefly use them for is to take a bulk of beer to a store about 12 miles off which we cannot reach by rail. On going to the station we generally take 30 to 40 barrels at a time. They often take 200 barrels a day. You must keep three men to go with the engine.'

However, horse-drawn drays remained the usual delivery method until the government's requisition of horses during the First World War necessitated the gradual introduction of motor transport.

Until the close of the last century Shep's produced only draught beer. In 1851 these were Stock Ale, Mild, Old, Stout, Porter, Old Strong and Table Beer. To take advantage of the most favourable brewing seasons beers intended for storing in casks in customers' cellars were brewed in March and October. October brewings would keep for 12 months, and those brewed in March kept through the summer.

The oak casks ranged from firkins to puncheons, pins not being used during the nineteenth century. The brewery's large cooperage continued until the advent of metal casks and the last cooper, Don Avery, retired in 1963. By the mid nineteenth century the brewery was supplying 383 private customers and 63 licensed trade outlets. By 1900 private accounts had peaked at about 1,000 and another 100 licensed outlets had been added.

Samuel Shepherd died in 1770 owning three pubs in Faversham. Today the brewery's estate of more than 370 pubs and Invicta Country Inns extends throughout Kent to Surrey, Sussex, London and Essex. And Shepherd Neame draught beers, such as Spitfire, are available in an increasing number of freehouses throughout the UK.

To cope with a demand for beer which has increased steadily during its history the brewery in Court Street has expanded considerably over the years. Yet it remains on its original site and blends harmoniously with its historic surroundings. It's also been extensively modernised. While visitors remain impressed with the nineteenth century teak mash tuns the rest of the brewery is as modern as any in the country.

In the late 1960s the company began an improvements programme which was to take 13 years and cost £2 million. This investment programme ended in March 1980 when the editor of the Daily Telegraph, and former cabinet minister, Bill (now Lord) Deedes opened the new brewhouse. Over the past five years more than £10 million has been invested in improving facilities at the brewery and increasing production capacity by 50 per cent. And while the latest statistics reveal that lager is vying with bitter for the title of Britain's most popular beer it is the traditional hoppy Kentish ales which have ensured that Shepherd Neame has survived and thrived through 13 reigns since William and Mary were on the throne.

This has been built on ales such as Master Brew Bitter, a cask-conditioned beer brewed with Kent's finest hops, and Bishops Finger, a powerful (abv 5.4 per cent) premium cask-conditioned ale brewed to a traditional Kentish recipe and named after a Kent wayside signpost that pointed pilgrims to Canterbury.

Spitfire Premium Bitter was launched in 1990 to support the RAF Benevolent Fund's 50th anniversary Battle of Britain Appeal – a fitting tribute to the survivors of the life-and-death struggle fought in the skies over Kent. The brewery presented the Appeal with a cheque for nearly £28,000.

At the 1994 Brewing Industry International Awards Spitfire won the gold medal for the world's best strong cask-conditioned ale – and Bishops Finger won the silver medal!

One of the latest additions to Shepherd Neame's 'fold' of real ales is Original Porter, a malt-rich winter warmer, dark in colour with heaps of flavours and added liquorice, along with three other seasonal ales – Early Bird in the spring, Goldings for summer and the autumnal Late Red.

Among the highlights of Shepherd Neame's 300th anniversary celebrations in 1998 was the visit of HRH The Prince of Wales who toured the brewery in the summer. Commenting after his tour Prince Charles praise Shepherd Neame for surviving and succeeding for so long.

Also in 1998 a special 1698 Celebration Ale was brewed and the official history of the company was published – *A Story that's been Brewing for 300 Years*.

As a sad post-script to this story, when Fremlins brewery across the road was closed in June 1991 it left only one major brewer in Faversham and, indeed, Kent. So, it's been left to Shepherd Neame to continue the county's brewing tradition into the next millennium.

And why not? They are, after all, Britain's oldest brewers.

STYLE OVER SUBSTANCE
The story of British lager

BY JEFF EVANS

Do you ever get the feeling that you've drawn the short straw? An essay on British lager for a book called Beer, Glorious Beer? It has to be a joke.

It is a commonly held belief amongst beer connoisseurs that British bottom-fermented beers – or 'lagers' as they are familiarly known in the UK – are generally not worth seeking out. Beer guru Michael Jackson has openly declared that he has never tasted a British lager for which he would cross the street. Flick through the pages of any international guide to beer and you'll find the British Isles are praised for their ales and stouts but there's barely a mention of lager. And yet lager now accounts for over 50 per cent of UK beer sales – a paradox needing explanation.

The story of British lager production dates back to the late 1800s, a few decades after production of lager was perfected in its native regions of Southern Germany and what was to become Czechoslovakia. The Industrial Revolution brought with it new refrigeration techniques and efficient transport links, enabling the Bavarian and Bohemian brewers to master their products, achieve consistency and exhibit their brews in wider markets. Their efforts were echoed around the world by other brewers, many of them of German or Czech stock themselves who had emigrated to the USA, Australia or the UK. Sometimes they saw a niche in brewing lager beers for their fellow immigrants – manual workers with a thirst to slake and a hankering for the type of beer they had left in their homelands. On other occasions, the brewers saw themselves almost as enlighteners, keen to share their beery passion with new neighbours who only had dark, heavy brews with which to relax. It was largely for this latter reason that Britain's first lager plant came into existence.

As Brian Glover recalls in his history of Welsh brewing, *Prince of Ales*, the North Wales brewing centre of Wrexham became the venue for the first foray into British bottom-fermented beer. In 1881, a group of German and Czech businessmen sought to woo local drinkers away from Welsh ales and onto their lighter continental brews. The Wrexham Lager Company was set up and took advantage of a well that gave forth a water similar in mineral content to that of Pilsen, the Bohemian birthplace of the pilsner style of beer. Despite changing hands and lurching through several financial difficulties, Wrexham continued at the forefront of British lager production until its take-over by Ind Coope & Allsopp in 1949, even exporting its wares to distant parts of the British Empire.

Similar moves were made in England, particularly through Allsopp's of Burton upon Trent, but far more successful were new enterprises in Scotland. Tennent of Glasgow and other breweries like John Jeffrey of Edinburgh, most employing immigrant brewers, steamed into production. From the start, the Scots made it one of their favourite tipples.

Roger Protz in *The Great British Beer Book* suggests that the Scottish taste for lager was perhaps down to a few reasons: that itinerant Scottish labourers returning from Europe brought with them an appetite for cooler, crisper beers; that the popular custom of drinking whisky chasers was more palatable with a lighter beer like lager; and that the lager of the day had much in common with contemporary Scottish pale ales that enjoyed longer fermentation periods at lower temperatures and were more lightly hopped than southern ales. Whatever the truth, Scottish lager brewing is still well to the fore today.

Elsewhere in Britain, though, lager was still appreciated only by a certain market – it was often sold by exclusive clubs and then became a 'woman's drink' – and the population as a whole remained loyal to 'British beer', especially during times of war, when anything with German connotations was regarded with suspicion. All that changed, however, when the accountants rose to the top of the brewing hierarchy in the 1960s.

The merger of Ind Coope, Tetley Walker and Ansells in 1961 to form Allied Breweries, and all the subsequent take-overs and closures that saw the establishment of the Big Six national breweries, confirmed the new emphasis on profit in the British brewing industry. The switch from traditional cask-conditioned ale to user-friendly, long-lasting keg beer has been well documented in other features. But part of the new equation was also lager.

Here was a product in the brewery portfolio that enjoyed only limited sales but which had PROFIT written all over it. In the 1960s and 1970s, a young generation of drinkers, liberated by the social changes of the post-war years and no longer tied to their parents' cultural apron strings, was looking for something new and different, a drink to call its own. Britons had also become less insular and started taking adventurous package holidays overseas, to places where they gained a taste for light, golden beers. Lager became the apple of the accountant's eye, especially when keg beer was derided into decline. Lager was novel, it had an exclusivity about it, it benefited from the German reputation for brewing excellence and could be sold at premium prices, even though it could be produced as cheaply as ordinary bitter. To ensure it was the name on everyone's lips the marketing men were set to work.

Progress was slow at first. From a one per cent market share in 1960, lager grew to seven per cent in 1971. Then the adverts began to take hold. Youths were seduced into thinking that it was manly to drink lager. It became the macho drink, the best way to pick up girls. Refreshing parts other beers couldn't reach, lager spawned a legion of Jack the Lads, following the bear, being a Skolar and always having a mate called Smith, as a host of new, low quality, high profit brands poured forth from the big breweries. There was no remorse at this debasement of a fine beer style. Indeed, continental breweries cheerfully complied with this act of indecency, allowing weaker, inferior copies of their award-winning beers to be brewed under licence in the UK. European visitors who fell into the trap of drinking beers whose names they knew from home were not amused. As pubs went Eurocrazy brewers added to the confusion by inventing bogus European titles for bogus European beers. Anyone looking for the original Hofmeister, Skol or Heldenbrau breweries, amongst others, would have combed the Continent in vain.

This lager boom was the archetypal triumph of style over substance. For however slick the advertising, the quality of these brews was generally recognised by genuine beer fans to be poor. Commercial pressures meant they were given little time to mature – or 'lager' – at the brewery (far from the standard six weeks-plus in Europe). They were not just filtered but pasteurised too, and, when they arrived in the pub, they were subjected to over-carbonation at the point of sale. There was scant regard for the German beer purity law – the Reinheitsgebot – which insisted that beer be brewed only from malt, hops, water and yeast, and no attention paid to continental brewers who claimed that a lager, because it is served chilled, needs an original gravity of at least 1040 to have any body or flavour. Standard British lagers weighed in at about 1033. Ironically, though, the increasing blandness and lack of character amongst beers of this style were an important plus point to the manufacturers. Kids fresh from lemonade need weaning on to stronger drink. These thin, fizzy, hunt-the-flavour lagers fitted the bill perfectly.

In the 1980s, the trend switched from ordinary lagers to premium or super-strength brews, when the first generation of lager boozers began to seek something more fulfilling. These products became just as widely criticised as their flimsier forebears, as an over-preoccupation with strength squeezed other attributes out of the picture. Another growth area in the 1980s was in 'New World' lagers. As well as brewing European brands under licence, British producers now added Australian, Canadian and American copies to their catalogues. These similarly failed to enchant the knowledgeable drinker, but maintained the attention of the younger consumer whose main consideration lay in drinking the beer with the right label (usually direct from a bottle) in a quest for street cred.

In fairness, there have been some notable exceptions to the 'British lager is bad' scenario. The regional breweries for instance, some producing under contract for an overseas concern, others soldiering on with their own lager brands, are considered to produce better lagers than their national rivals. Alastair Hook, a Germany-trained brewer, puts it down to preserving their reputation: 'The regionals take pride in their ales, so they're not going to neglect their other products', he reckons, and that is why they probably buy better ingredients, allow longer conditioning at the brewery and ensure a reasonable alcohol content. McMullen of Hertford, Samuel Smith of Tadcaster and Young's of London are just three regionals which have persevered with their own lager brands in the face of opposition from the mass-advertised names.

Anyone glancing through the history book of British lager will recognise two focal points: its birth and its renaissance. The former, as has been said, was largely about cultural heritage, honest attempts to recreate a classic beer style and, in some instances, a response to market demand. The latter, on the other hand, was entirely profit driven. It aimed to establish (and succeeded in establishing) a new culture, by bastardising a classic beer style and whipping up popular interest. The quality of the product played second fiddle to image and financial return, and in this respect the story of British lager epitomises some of the worst excesses of the British brewing industry as a whole.

Little wonder, therefore, that connoisseur beer guides ignore British lager and little wonder that the mention of British lager in the same breath as Beer, Glorious Beer is a source of amusement.

WELSH BEER
The unsung secret

BY BRIAN GLOVER

When people conjure up images of Wales they imagine dramatic scenery, towering castles, coal mines, rugby players and male voice choirs echoing down the valleys. They rarely think of beer.

Yet what slaked the thirst of the miners up from the pit face? What satisfied the prop forward, muddy from the scrum? What lubricated the throats of the massed ranks of singers? The answer is beer.

But while Ireland bragged about its famous stout, England its Burton ales and Scotland its heavy export brews, Wales generally kept quiet about its heady heritage. The people's lips were sealed – round a pint glass.

In part this was due to the power of the chapels and the strong temperance movement. The Welsh brewing industry fermented in a much drier land than the rest of Britain. In England the campaigners against alcohol held rallies, addressed meetings and argued strongly for restrictive legislation. In Wales they lived next door. Nowhere else in Britain did their beliefs take such a profound hold.

During a temperance crusade in Tredegar in 1859, led by the teetotal advocate 'Cheap John', seven thousand signed the pledge. That summer the receipts of the local Rhymney Brewery plunged by £500 a month. Pubs, and even breweries, buckled under the pressure and closed. Those that survived tended to keep their heads down behind the bar. No nation boasted less about their beer than the Welsh.

Yet at one time Welsh Ale had been highly valued throughout Britain.

When King Ine of Wessex drew up a set of laws between AD 690 and 693 one of them referred to payments in kind in return for land. The law ruled that for every ten hides the food rent should include '12 ambers of Welsh ale'. Almost 500 years later the drink was still much sought after. Coelred, Abbot of Medehamstede (Peterborough), granted his tenant Wulfred a church estate in return for goods including 'five mittan of Welsh ale'.

This special ale was a strong, heavy brew laced with expensive spices like cloves, cinnamon and ginger. Sometimes it was sweetened with honey. Known as 'bragawd' or 'bragot', it was much more prized than the standard ale or 'cwrw' used for everyday drinking. But, as unscrupulous brewers began to adulterate this potent pot with less desirable ingredients, so laws were passed that ale be brewed only from malt, yeast and water (even hops were banned for a while). Wales's early claim to brewing fame became just a distant hangover.

It was not until the nineteenth century that the dragon's drop breathed fire again – in the unlikely scenic setting of Llangollen in North Wales. Walter Booth's brewery gained such a reputation for its strong ales that they were sold by agents throughout England. George Borrow, in his popular account of a tour round 'Wild Wales' in 1854, smacked his lips at the thought of Llangollen 'which is celebrated for its ale all over Wales'.

The sweet smell of success did not last long. The brewery was badly hit by fire in 1870 and taken over by a London brewer, John Tanqueray. But, by then, the small tourist town was already overshadowed by its much larger neighbour, Wrexham.

Chronicler Alfred Barnard, in his monumental work, *The Noted Breweries of Great Britain and Ireland,* declared in 1892: 'Wrexham may now be called the Burton of Wales.' Like the famous Staffordshire ale capital, the Welsh town had ideal water for brewing. Its foundations were built on beer. By the late 1860s Wrexham boasted 19 commercial breweries. The trade dominated the town. In the first 50 years after its incorporation as a borough in 1857 brewers accounted for more than a third of the mayors.

Business was helped by the fact that the bustling town was home to a large army garrison. One Victorian wag claimed: 'Wrexham beer is made from mashed sheet music and boxing gloves, for it makes one either sing or fight.' An appreciative visitor in 1860 reported: 'Two or more glasses made us feel quite patriotic and in good humour with everybody.' It was strong stuff. The enticing taste was even blamed for making the Chester to Shrewsbury stagecoach run late!

The emphasis was on quality rather than quantity, with many breweries noted for producing specialist beers. Thompson's Sun and Eagle Breweries in Abbot Street concentrated on strong ales under the slogan 'Cwrw Da Am Byth' (Good Beer For Ever). Chadwick's Burton Brewery in Bridge Street took pride in its 'Y Stowt Cymreig Pûr' (Celebrated Welsh Stout).

But even Wrexham, where the authorities once ran a preacher out of town for denouncing the evils of strong drink, could not escape the fervent force of the religious and temperance revivals. The nonconformist chapels and teetotal movements were inextricably linked in Wales, and in 1881 demonstrated their political power by forcing through the Welsh Sunday Closing Act, which shuts pubs on the holy day.

Welsh breweries saw which way the steam was blowing and, fearing total prohibition in the Principality, eased back on the malt in the mash tun. Frederic Soames, who ran the largest brewery in Wrexham, told beer chronicler Barnard that when he took over the Nag's Head Brewery in 1879 he 'determined to brew a light, thoroughly finished beer ... because such ale was bound to assist the cause of real temperance.'

He was seeking to brew a lower-alcohol ale which would be less likely to offend the campaigners on the water wagon. He succeeded. In 1931 Soames merged with the nearby Island Green Brewery and Dorsett Owen of Oswestry to form Border Breweries, which was known for its range of low gravity milds and bitters. Only one Border brew, the bottled Royal Wrexham Barley Wine, reflected the town's staggering past.

In South Wales the draught story was drawn on different lines, reinforced by the demands of the massed ranks of miners and steel workers for a refreshing, cheap brew to quench their raging thirsts. In some valleys the preference was for light-coloured beers, usually known as PAs, and in others for dark ales, but their common characteristic was that they were relatively weak. Breweries needing a stronger beer usually bought in a pale ale from Burton, like Bass.

These bread-and-butter brews steadily declined in strength over the years. Fenvale Brewery of Pontygwaith in the Rhondda was brewing just one draught beer in 1960, a light SPA of 1031 gravity. Henry Holder, one of the last head brewers at Rhymney Brewery, recalled that the company produced two draught beers: Golden Hopped Bitter (1036) and Pale Mild Ale (1030). The weak PMA was by far the best seller, averaging 1,750 barrels a week compared to 250 for GHB.

Welsh breweries which ventured beyond these basic brews were few and far between. David Williams's Taff Vale Brewery in Merthyr Tydfil tried to break out of this weak beer barrel in the early 1890s, commenting in

1893: 'Some five years ago nothing else but fresh beers were practically consumed, namely cheap XX, but within the last three years the firm has been working up a large quantity of better quality beers.'

Brains of Cardiff was so unusual in developing its own 'Burton Ale' that Barnard thought it worth comment: 'Messrs Brain and Co. have now become so proficient in the art of brewing pale ales that the Cardiff publicans are not obliged to go to the "beer city" for their Burton ales, the commodity being now brewed on the same principle in their own town.' Despite this development Brain's best-selling beer for most of its history was the low-gravity Red Dragon dark.

Even when South Wales's brewers produced so-called 'strong ales' in a bottle they were notoriously weak. The term had become so discredited by the 1920s that Buckley's of Llanelli advertised their bottled strong ale under the slogan 'The Strong Ale that IS strong'. Even then it wasn't. It was just less weak than the others.

Wales's taste for low-gravity – but often surprisingly tasty – beers remains to this day. The market may have moved up to mid-strength brews like Brains Bitter, Buckleys Best and Hancocks HB, but the demand for a refreshing session beer remains strong.

Darker brews, like Brains Dark and Worthington Dark, are still popular. Lighter, hoppy ones, like Felinfoel Bitter and CPA, from the former clubs' brewery, Crown of Pontyclun, have keen local followings. The country's two major brands are Allbright, from Welsh Brewers, and Welsh Bitter, from Whitbread (both 3.2% alcohol). Both processed beers reflect in style and strength the traditional, light-coloured PAs which once dominated the packed pubs and clubs trade.

Only in recent years have stronger brews, like Brains SA and Felinfoel Double Dragon (both 4.2%), taken prominent positions on the bar while some colourful new breweries have revived Wales's ancient tradition for powerful ales, notably the dangerously drinkable Son of a Bitch (6%) from Bullmastiff Brewery of Cardiff.

Crown Buckley even named their premium ale Reverend James after one of the original pulpit-preaching pioneers of Buckley's Brewery. The title recalled a time when the gospel and the glass went hand in hand before the temperance tide sapped the strength of Welsh ale.

Now the body of the beer is rising again – sadly at a time when the body of the Welsh brewing industry is close to rolling in the grave.

In 1997 Brains merged with Crown Buckley resulting in the closure of Buckleys Brewery in Llanelli. At the same time Bass announced that their

South Wales brewery, Hancock's in Cardiff, was to close. In North Wales the last rites were read on another historic site when Carlsberg-Tetley decided that their Wrexham lager Brewery was to stop brewing.

This leaves just two long-standing Welsh breweries – Brains of Cardiff and Felinfoel of Llanelli with Brains closing their Old Brewery in 1999 and taking over Hancock's site. But there is still life in the drained glass.

These two survivors have been joined in flying the flag for traditional Welsh beer by a handful of new breweries, like Bullmastiff, the Plassey Brewery near Wrexham, and Tomos Watkin of Llandeilo.

SCOTLAND'S CASK ALE REVIVAL

BY ALLAN M^CLEAN

The barman in the Glasgow pub sneered when I asked if he sold any cask-conditioned beer.

'What? Real ale? Naw. Nae demand for it here,' he replied with an expression on his face which seemed to imply: 'We've got a right one here.'

I encountered that pub again recently. It had a big sign outside inviting passers-by to come in and enjoy the wide range of real ales. Another notice indicated proudly that the pub specialised in cask-conditioned. The only reason I didn't go in for a drink was that I had arranged to meet a pal in one of half-a-dozen other real ale pubs in the vicinity. The difference between those two experiences of the same place was five years and a remarkable change of attitude in between.

At one time there was no real ale in Glasgow. Drinkers of proper draught had to catch a train 12 miles to Bishopton on the line to Gourock. Now cask beer is widely available in the city, although there is a belief elsewhere that Glasgow is not a good market for real ale. Lager has been brewed in Glasgow by Tennents since 1885 and this has tended to colour people's expectations. Intriguingly, those pubs which have tried real ale have found there is a demand, even in lager land. Some unlikely-looking Glasgow pubs have cask ale on sale, and not just those catering for students or middle-class trendies.

For me, the arrival of real ale in Glasgow is a clear sign that proper beer has arrived back in Scotland at last. For a long time Edinburgh was regard-

Pubs of the Cotswolds and the Thames Valley
by Mark Turner

The Eight Bells, Eaton, Oxfordshire.

The Crown at Cookham, Berks.

The Perch and Pike, South Stoke, Oxfordshire.

The Catherine Wheel, Goring, Oxfordshire.

The Black Boy, Hurley, Berkshire.

The Trout Inn, Lower Wolvercote, Oxford.

The Greyhound, Wargrave, Berkshire.

The Plough Inn, Kelmscot, Gloucestershire.

Inn Signs of England
by Neil Holmes and Barry Pepper

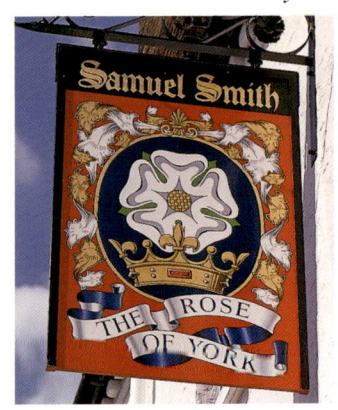

Ham, Nr Richmond, Surrey.

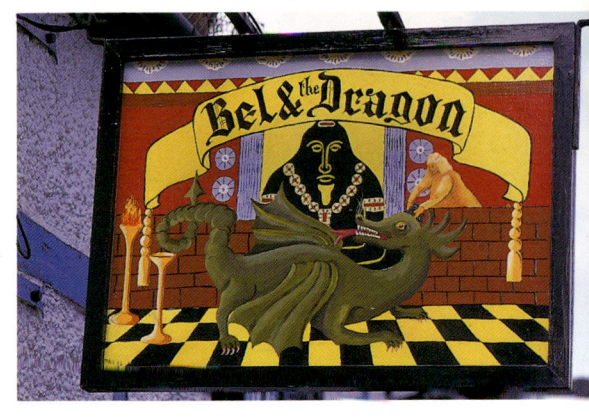

Cookham, Berks.

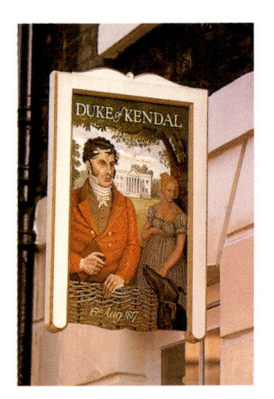

Duke of Kendal,
38 Connaught Street,
London, W2.

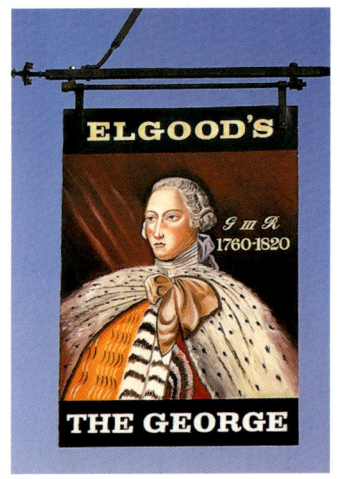

Doddington, Cambs.

Morlands Brewery Plaque, Oxon.

Weymouth, Dorset.

The Two Chairmen. Victorian pub sign.

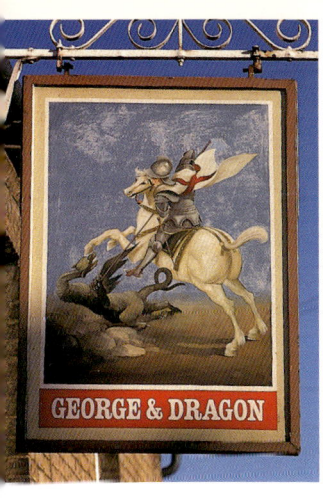

George and Dragon, Littleport, Cambs.

London Porterhouse, King's Lynn, Norfolk.

Great Massingham, Norfolk.

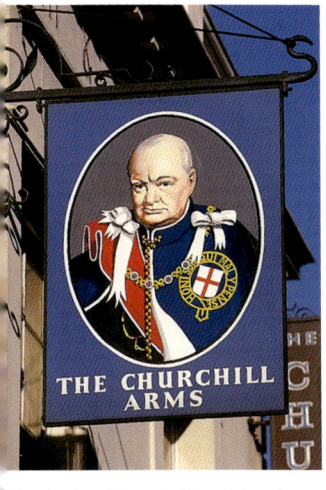

Kensington Church Street, London.

Above: Thornham, Norfolk. Below right: Reigate, Surrey.

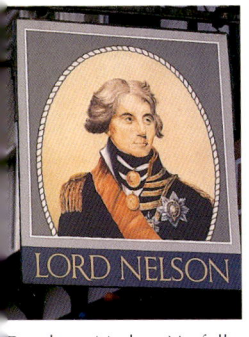

Burnham Market, Norfolk.

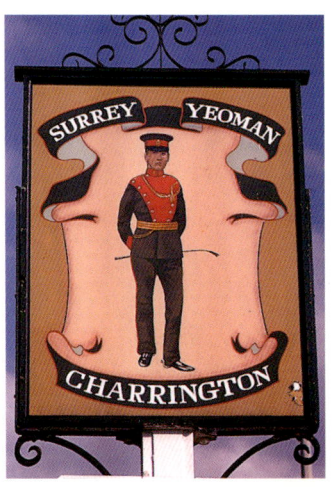

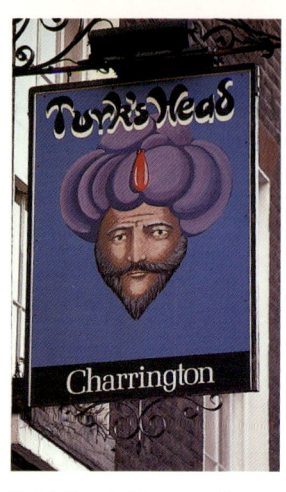

Turk's Head, Kinnerton Street, London, SW1.

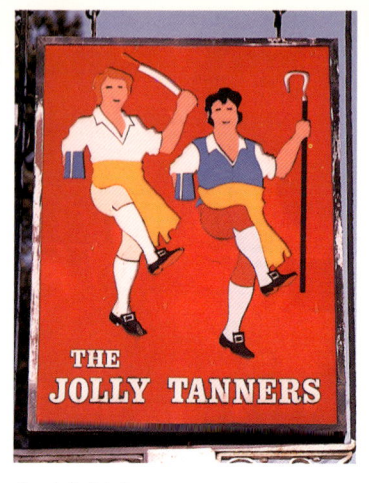

Staplefield, Sussex.

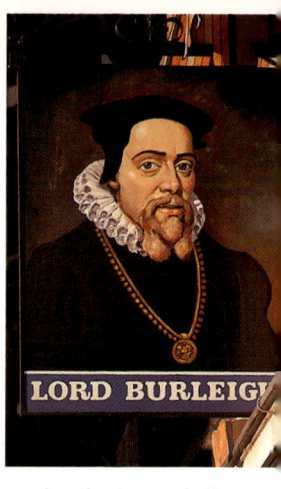

Lord Burleigh, Vauxhall Bridge Road, SW1.

Hunslet, Leeds.

Ye Olde Spotted Horse, Putney.

Mortal Man, Troutbeck Cumbria.

The Sun, Dent, Cumbria.

Starbotton, North Yorks.

Greyhound, Market Square, Blandford Forum.

Red Lion, Market Square, Blandford Forum.

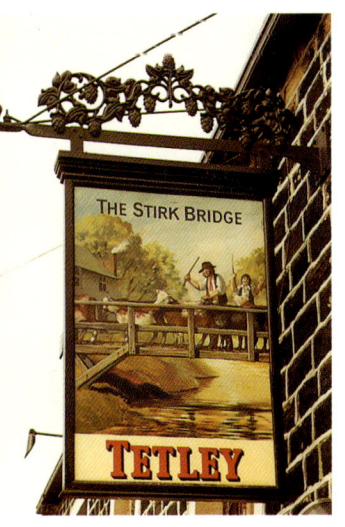

Stirk Bridge, Sowerby Bridge, West Yorks.

Beaumont Arms, Kirkheaton, West Yorks.

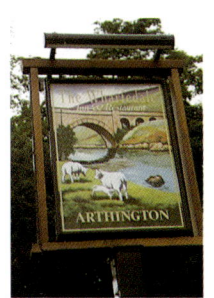

Wharfedale, Arthington, West Yorks.

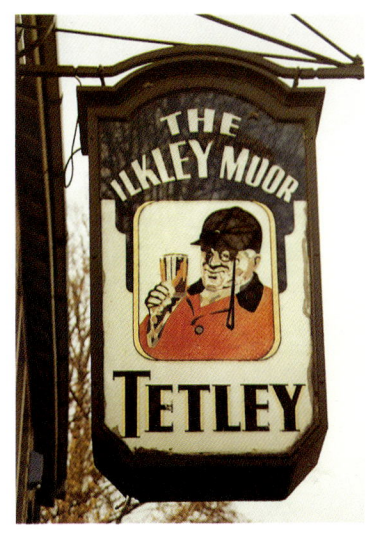

Ilkley Moor Vaults, Ilkley.

The sign on the former Chequers on the Hambleton Drovers' Road.

Otley, West Yorks.

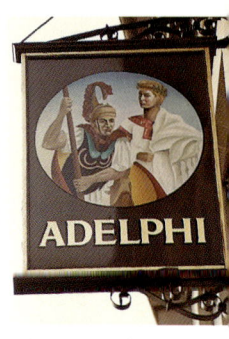

Adelphi, Leeds.

Rose and Crown, Romaldkirk, Co.Durham.

Pickering, North Yorks.

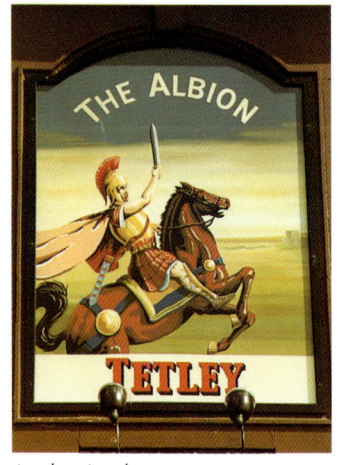

Armley, Leeds.

Tadcaster, North Yorks.

ed as the ale heartland, with odd pockets elsewhere, including Aberdeen. Now, although it is not everywhere, real ale is certainly very widely available. On one occasion I was astounded to find a remarkable choice in a remote Highland pub in the middle of nowhere, all sold in good condition to appreciative hill-walkers and climbers who worked up a thirst in the mountains. (But I do not recommend standing on a table to conduct the community singing. I left that pub with one leg in plaster.)

Yet, when I was first learning how to drink 30 years ago, decent beer was disappearing faster than I could find it. Even in Edinburgh we almost lost the last of the smooth stuff you could taste without having fizzy bubbles blast the tongue. Part of the ale revival has involved the invasion of English brews; something which would have been unheard of in the old days, with certain distinguished exceptions such as Draught Bass and Worthington White Shield. Now, there is a steadily increasing choice of Scottish ales to enjoy, including one-off varieties offered for just a few weeks at a time, something many English breweries are doing, too.

After a spate of brewery closures in the 1960s the safeguarding of real ale was largely down to Scotland's only two remaining independent breweries of any size, Maclay's of Alloa and Belhaven of Dunbar. Since those days both have extended the number of real ales they produce most impressively. Maclays Oat Malt Stout uses malted oats, as its name implies, and marks the restoration of a Victorian recipe (although it does not include the linseed which featured in the original, which seems to have been designed partly as a laxative, whereas today's version is intended to refresh without reaching parts we would rather not reach.) and Kane's Amber is a welcome tribute by Maclays to the late Dan Kane, a CAMRA activist. Among 1990s additions to the Belhaven ale range is Sandy Hunter's Traditional Ale, named after a former chairman, a remarkable honour in his own lifetime for one of Scotland's best loved brewers.

Scottish and Newcastle retained some real ale in the 1970s, but only in a few pubs whose licensees have insisted on continuing to stock it because they knew how to look after ale and enjoyed it themselves. Ind Coope killed off cask and so did Tennents, which has now become the Scottish subsidiary of Bass. Of the big boys Ind Coope, in its later guises as Allied, Alloa Brewery and Carlsberg-Tetley Alloa, acquired the best name for enthusiastically bringing back real ale. Much of this has been in guest form from other breweries, including ones in the same group, but Arrol's 80/- is brewed in Alloa.

S and N looked like getting a good record too, but this was somewhat dented when the corner-cutting of mass-production at the Fountain Brewery in Edinburgh began to show through in unsatisfactory tastes in the flagship McEwans 80/-. I detected a change of heart at S and N, most notably in the re-launch in the summer of 1995 of William Younger's No. 3, involving a return to the original recipe for this remarkably improved ale. Competition from other brewers seem to have finally encouraged S and N to get better and I welcome that wholeheartedly because it was a William Younger's beer I first fell in love with at the age of 16 back in 1963. Sadly they have now discontinued it.

Tennents dragged their feet somewhat. But the eventual realisation that Draught Bass and guest ales from various Scottish and English independent breweries were selling well encouraged the production in 1994 of the first cask ale at Tennent's Wellpark Brewery in Glasgow since the 1960s. An earlier trial at Tennent's Heriot Brewery in Edinburgh flopped through lack of enthusiasm by the company. Then the Heriot Brewery itself closed. The revived cask from Wellpark is, strange though it may seem, named after the closed Aitkin's Brewery of Falkirk instead of carrying Tennent's own name.

But probably the most significant development in the Scottish ale scene was the decision in the late 1980s by Vaux of Sunderland to close its last subsidiary in Scotland, Lorimer and Clark, whose Caledonian Brewery in Edinburgh had remained virtually unchanged since 1869. This closure plan turned into good news, because the management buy-out team which saved the Caledonian Brewery then went on to build up a portfolio of some of the greatest bottled and cask ales to be produced anywhere.

Scotland also enjoys a selection of small brewers who have only come into business since the early 1980s. Several false starts saw independents open and shut, but others stayed in business. The most northerly is the Orkney Brewery, whose fine ales with names redolent of the islands' Viking past, are now to be discovered all over the United Kingdom despite the distances involved.

The highest village in the north of Scotland, Tomintoul – famed for the property bought there by an accountant who made millions by fiddling the Metropolitan Police – is another outpost with its own brewery. (No direct connection with the police accountant, though.) And there is the Borve Brewhouse north of Aberdeen. Ken Brooker, a former Ford area sales manager, has been working wonders with his Harviestoun Brewery on a farm at Dollar, near Alloa. Glasgow even acquired its own ale micro brewer and other small newcomers have sprung up in Scotland.

The biggest of the new Scottish independents, and also the oldest, coming up for half way through its second decade, is Broughton Brewery in Border country. Greenmantle Ale associates it with the Broughton author, John Buchan. There are other distinctive brews from Broughton, which has expanded impressively. Broughton's Scottish Oatmeal Stout is one of the tasty ones.

BEER AND BREWING IN IRELAND

BY CAROLYNNE PEPPER

It is more then 25 years ago that I had my first taste of beer, and not just any beer either but Guinness Stout. My recollection of that taste is rather mixed, bearing in mind that I had just given birth to a set of twin boys, and all I was really bothered about was to make sure I was able to give a good healthy start to my tiny sons for the next six weeks was the most vulnerable stage of their lives. The medical profession advised me as with all mothers of multiple births to drink a pint of stout a day because its nutritious value not only helps mother's milk, but helps mother to get over the shock of having more babies to look after rather then just one! I'm not certain whether this rather enriched beginning has any bearing on the fact that I now have two six foot strapping lads, who have since become real ale drinkers and not lager louts, but it has certainly done them no harm. In the past there was a term 'nursing mothers' whose role it was to help suckle babies whose mothers were too ill to perform this duty and that they were paid handsomely for doing this and drinking porter or stout was important to them also.

It was many years later on my first visit to Ireland with my then future husband, who had previously spent many a happy time in this wonderful country drinking the black stuff, that I got to drink a real pint of Guinness. Our many Irish friends say to this day that the first drink of stout on Irish soil is the best, I would not argue the fact and I am sure that whatever your preferences are in Irish stout, as there are several to choose from, your first sip is magic. Several visits later I started to look more deeply into the background of Irish stout, and found it historically interesting and tied very much into the history of English brewing.

Brewing began around 432 AD when St Patrick landed in Ireland with his followers and among his entourage was his own brewer, a priest called Mescan. Also mentioned was St Brigid who brewed ale at Easter time to supply all the churches in her neighbourhood. Another record is in a book of the ancient laws of Ireland, *Seanchus Mor*, printed in 441 AD where the Irish name for ale is *coirm* which was made with barley, and the liquor from it was called *courmi*. There are many references made to the growing of barley and the production of malt and the tests for malt. The climate in Ireland was congenial to growing barley and wheat and they soon discovered the art of brewing which was mainly done by the women on farms.

In twelfth-century Dublin, along the River Poddle, where the water was good enough for brewing, a considerable amount of ale was brewed by women and in the *Chain Book of the Dublin Corporation* reference is made to laws prescribing the duties of women-brewers which were laid down by the city's Common Council during the fourteenth century. In the fifteenth century a brewery was established at Enniscorthy in County Wexford by George Killian Lett producing the first recorded brewing of Irish Ale which was ruby coloured. The brewery closed in 1956, but appears to have had a popular following in other countries and beers under this name are sold by Pelforth in France, Coors in the United States and Heineken in the Netherlands. The original brewery building is still standing but sadly now without its waterwheel.

Barnaby Rych in his *New Description of Ireland* written in 1610 gave a full account of the brewing industry of Dublin. Later, in the reign of Charles II, it was estimated that Dublin had 1,180 ale houses and 91 brew houses for a population of 4,000 families. Apart from these public sources, the affluent society also set up brewing plants in their mansions for their own consumption. Much of this private practice died out during the eighteenth century and brewing slowly passed to the common brewers which had been incorporated in Dublin by a Royal Charter in 1696. One such private brewer was a young man named Arthur Guinness whose father, Richard Guinness, brewed for the Bishop of Cashel in the early eighteenth century. The Bishop died in 1752 and in his will he left the young Arthur the princely sum of £100 with which he set up an ale brewery in Leixlip in County Kildare.

Some folk say that Arthur Guinness brewed his immortal porter by accident by burning the malted barley with the caramelised result giving a much darker and better tasting drink, though others said that the recipe was stolen from the monks, or that there was magic in the water of the River Liffey. But whatever the reason it was the start of young Arthur Guinness's career in the brewing industry.

It was during this period that the import of English style porter was making inroads into Ireland and threatening the very existence of Irish brewing that Arthur Guinness considered seriously setting up a brewery in Wales to overcome the disadvantages of paying the excessive Irish duty. However as events turned out in 1759 he took a 9,000 year lease on a disused brewery at St James's Gate in Dublin for an annual rent of £45.

In 1762 duty on beer brewed in Ireland was 5s.6d per barrel as against one shilling for every imported barrel of Porter. The imports of Porter rose from 28,935 barrels to 58,675 in 1773 and the number of breweries in Dublin had fallen from 70 to 30. Shortly afterwards Arthur Guinness decided to stop the production of Irish ale and concentrate on porter, and employed a reputable London brewer to perfect the production. His last brew of ale was on 1st April, 1799.

New legislation in 1777 gave relief on Irish excise duty and this resumed the confidence in the Irish brewing industry which resulted in imports falling off. The expansion of Guinness Porter in Ireland was done by using the natural transport facilities available to the brewery, first by canal and river then later by building a private railway to connect with the existing state railway system. This helped increase home trade and also exports. In 1816 1,000 barrels of Porter went abroad, most of it from Guinness.

Arthur Guinness only lived to see part of this resurgence and much of the expansion happened during his son's period. Arthur Guinness II changed the style of the Porter. He cut costs and to avoid paying the unnecessary English taxes he used some tax free unmalted and roasted barley with the regular malt to give it the distinguished dry quality and bitter taste which became recognised as Guinness Stout. Over the years this has become an international product, brewed under licence across the world, drunk by many a famous celebrity, and celebrated in poems and songs.

Other Irish breweries have developed over the centuries, the oldest known being Smithwick's in Kilkenny. Smithwick's have been brewing on the site of a Franciscan Abbey since 1710 where records show that the monks of the abbey were brewing in the 14th century. Part of the abbey still stands in the shadow of the more modern facilities.

Brewing at Kilkenny went on from 1710 right through the turbulent years of the United Irishmens' Rebellion in 1798, through the Great Famine during the nineteenth century and the 1916 uprising, From1851 until 1873 the brewery had become the largest one outside Dublin and Cork. It increased output and developed an export trade to the ports of Wales and south west England. During this period eight different beers were produced which included ales, porter and stout. Porter brewing ceased in 1918. The Irish brewing industry had a lean period in the first half of the new century after Britain blocked Irish imports because British brewers had established a tied house system, which meant that Smithwick's were forced to consolidate and concentrate on the home market. Much of this was in and around Kilkenny. In 1944 the company expanded by building a network with its own transport to distribute ale throughout the 32 counties of Ireland, not an easy task with the competition of other established Irish breweries. In spite of the difficulty, by 1953, Smithwick's name was known nation-wide and demand outstripped production so the purchase of the Old Great Northern Brewery in Dundalk enabled it to continue. In 1956 Smithwick's became a public company, and the Guinness Brewing Company became a major shareholder eventually taking control of the group in 1964. Smithwick's Ale, the major product, is very much in the typical Irish style with a reddish tinge and sweet tasting. The brewery at Dundalk, still brewing for Smithwick's now concentrates on three products: Smithwick's Barley Wine, Cherry's Ale and Macardle's Ale.

Cork is another well established brewing centre with two breweries, Beamish and Crawford and Murphys. There is a religious division. Beamish and Crawford's original owners were Scottish Protestants from Northern Ireland. They were landowners who exported beef and butter into the south. The brewery situated on the River Lee, was always thought of the Protestant brewery, and claims to be the oldest brewer of porter and stout in Ireland. Murphy's brewery which is on the north side of the city, was built in 1856 by four brothers from a staunchly Roman Catholic family on the site of an orphans' hospital which also had a well consecrated to Our Lady, and which now is a religious shrine. The facade of Ladyswell Brewery resembles an Edwardian railway station.

In Northern Ireland, Belfast is the only city to have a history of brewing which started when John Bell opened a brewery in Hercules Street in 1800. Clotworthy Dobbin also started brewing Dobbin's Ale in the same street in 1810. The sites of both breweries are now part of the city's main street, Royal Avenue. Mr Dobbin moved his brewery to Smithfield Market Square in 1824 and it remained there until 1897. In 1860 he employed a brewer,

Thomas R Caffrey, who three years later married his younger daughter and took over the family business in 1865 when Mr Dobbin died. Thomas Caffrey moved the brewery to a larger site in West Belfast which was officially opened in 1901 as the Mountain Brewery, having the Black Mountain in its background. Most of the original equipment was moved from Smithfield to the new brewery, including the two 100 barrel copper kettles which remained in use and on the premises until 1974 when they were replaced by two 150 barrel stainless steel kettles. The main product that came from this brewery was Caffrey's Treble X stout, which had its own distinct style.

In 1950 the brewery ceased trading as Thomas R Caffrey and Sons and lay dormant until a consortium was formed and started trading as The Ulster Brewery Company producing a range of local ales. During the early 1960s, the brewery underwent many changes of names until in 1974 it was bought by Bass trading as Bass Ireland.

The only other breweries in Northern Ireland at present are micro plants in County Antrim and County Down. Hilden Brewery, set in the grounds of a Georgian country house near Lisburn has been producing real ale since 1981. It started by supplying one local pub, but now, as there has been a resurgence of traditional ale in Northern Ireland, it has a number of other customers both in the province and in England. The Whitewater Brewery in Kilkeel started brewing in 1996 and sends out a range of traditional beers to a dozen or more outlets in Northern Ireland.

The independent brewery business in the Republic has exploded in recent years. At Inagh in west Clare I spent a Christmas eve afternoon effortlessly supping Black Biddy Stout in the Biddy Early brewery, I was warned by the brewer not to drink too much as it has an aphrodisiac effect on women and needless to say I took heed of his warning, especially as I was just given the keys of the car which always has a sobering effect on me. Sadly Padraig Garvey who pioneered the renaissance of real ale into the south died in 1998 but his sons have taken over. And his courageous lead has been followed up by a number of others. Best known is the Porterhouse Brewing Company in Dublin a brewery set in the centre of a pub that was once a warehouse close to the River Liffey and not too far from the Guinness factory. After taking the BIIA award for the best stout it now advertises the claim, 'Dublin's Second Largest Brewery Brews the World's Best Stout.'

Nine others have also taken on the big companies in small plants from Cork, Newbridge, Enfield, Roscommon, Thurles, Carlow and three in

Dublin. With Biddy Early and Porterhouse they have formed the Independent Irish Brewers Guild and competition is rife once more in Erin's green and pleasant land.

MANCHESTER ALE

BY GRAHAM LEES

When beer and brewing in Britain are discussed, Burton-on-Trent, London, or Edinburgh always seem to figure first as centres of style or output linked to the great thirst for beer which began in the early nineteenth century. Manchester is remembered as the place where cotton was spun in a thousand dark, satanic mills. But greater Manchester probably created more breweries and pubs than anywhere else in Britain to lubricate the industrial revolution. And it is the last great British city still to boast five breweries with roots firmly embedded in that period. From the late eighteenth century, hundreds of thousands of people poured into the greater Manchester region to power the cotton mills, coal mines and engineering factories.

Between 1774 and 1837, the population of the old city of Manchester alone swelled by nearly 700 per cent, from 41,000 to nearly 275,000. The incomers were a mixture of English rural poor and European immigrants and entrepreneurs. (Some of the profits from a Manchester factory established by Frederick Engel's German family kept Karl Marx in beer money while he mused over his communist manifesto at the British Museum in London.)

By 1836 there were 4,574 brewers and beer retailers in Manchester, excluding hundreds of 'hush shops' – illegal beer houses where supping was just as frenetic, but also cheaper. The import of raw cotton in the early nineteenth century illustrates just how much of a thirst must have been generated. In 1807, 196,000 bales arrived from north America; by 1837 more than 1,000,000 bales a year were needed to fuel the mills.

The hot and sweaty conditions of those mills doubtless spawned the Manchester beer taste which today is quenchingly dry and hoppy. Today's pale bitter beers and pale and dark milds are the descendants of the porters and dark brown ales which both nourished the bodies and numbed the minds of Manchester's overworked poor. Every street corner had its alehouse, every district its brewery.

Keen-eyed travellers through greater Manchester today will spot numerous brewery names etched into pub walls and glass: Threlfall, Wilson, Oldham, Chester, Groves & Whitnall, Swales, Cornbrook. Many more names have disappeared altogether – Chadwicks, Pollards, Woodside, Walker & Homfreys, McKenna's, Hardy's to name just a few. Some are long since gone, others succumbed within only the last ten years: Oldham, bought and closed by Boddingtons; Threlfall-Chesters, closed by Whitbread; Wilsons, closed by whoever happened to own the Watney conglomerate at the time.

But there is still much to be cheerful about: the thriving breweries of Boddingtons (founded 1778), Lees (1828), Robinson's (1838), Holt (1849), and Hyde's (1863) produce more than 25 distinctive draught and bottled beers.

The classic Victorian redbrick pile of John Willie Lees (no relation) at Middleton Junction owes its existence in more ways than one to the cotton industry. Ex-mill owner John Lees got bored with cosy retirement and noting the growing demand for beer he bought a row of cottages and converted them into a small brewery to produce ale and porter. The present, expanded brewery buildings were commissioned by John's grandson in 1876 and some of the current brewing equipment – virtual museum pieces – date from that time. Much of Lees's beers are still served from wooden casks.

The most popular beer in the 175 Lees pubs is the dry, hoppy Bitter (4.2 abv), but the family is committed to producing its dark Mild (3.5), even though it is a declining style. A strong winter ale, the fruity Moonraker (7%) stiffens the draught portfolio. Harvest Ale (11.5), is a bottled-only beer made in November from the current year's harvest of barley and hops. It is vintage dated and matures well for several years, acquiring port-like qualities. Brewer Giles Dennis describes Harvest as a 'desire to show the world the best of British brewing'.

Robinson's originally slaked the thirst of the hatmakers of Stockport, where the brewery still stands. It's the biggest of the greater Manchester independents with an estate of 409 pubs. They recently renamed their draught ales and expanded the range to six. The pale brown Mild is now Hatters (3.3 abv), the ordinary bitter is called Old Stockport (3.5 abv), and a new premium bitter takes the name of the first brewing Robinson: Frederics (5% abv). The brewery's biggest seller is simply called Best Bitter (4.2 abv), an apple-fruity amber ale with a moreish dry finish. But Robinson's is perhaps best known for its powerful old ale, Old Tom (8.5 abv), brewed since 1899 and sold on draught only during the winter months. It's not a beer to trifle with.

Holt's – a stone's throw from Boddingtons Brewery and close to the city centre – is something of an eccentric, but much loved family firm. They maintain a very low profile behind brewery walls not quite as tall as those of the nearby Strangeways Prison with the landmark phallic chimney. Holt's beers send a shudder through folk unaccustomed to uncompromisingly bitter beer, but there is a strong cult following from aficionados, who have playfully nicknamed the brewery Drabs. The Bitter ale (4% abv) boasts 40 units of bitterness, and even the dark Mild (3.2) is comparatively bitter and dry. Holt's don't exhibit and they strictly control their beer in the free trade with carefully selected outlets. Until recently they wouldn't let their beer travel more than 50 miles. They spurn promotion but turnover in their own 100 or so pubs is so big they can deliver in huge hogsheads – 54-gallon casks which have all but disappeared elsewhere in Britain. Prices at just over £1 a pint might be a factor too.

All this would have met with the approval of Joseph, who was the son of an early-nineteenth-century weaver and knew what his customers wanted. He was egged on by a tough wife who rolled up her sleeves to better the family's fortunes. Holt's is also noted for maintaining a number of unspoilt classic Edwardian pubs of dark mahogany wood and etched glass. Good examples can be found in Eccles and Prestwich.

On the other side of the city centre is the smallest of the surviving old Mancunian brewing fraternity. Hyde's holds the record for the number of flits. Between 1863 and 1899, the family moved their brewing operations five times around the city. Poor water supply, inadequate buildings and tenancy problems might have persuaded Hyde's to give up and perhaps return to the coal mining business from whence they came. But the Hyde story is also one of female doggedness in a man's world. Annie Hyde ran the family business for 56 years from the age of 21 until her death in 1936, steering it through economic slumps and periods of expansion. Hyde's own 60 pubs, including a few in north Wales which they bought protectively when

Manchester city council embarked on a deliberate policy in the late 1940s to reduce pub licences. They brew four regular draught beers, two of which are pale and dark mild ales (3.5 abv). A third brew, simply – and perhaps misleadingly – labelled Light (3.7 abv) is sometimes taken to be a mild, but it would shame many so-called Bitters elsewhere. The best selling 'Bitter' (3.8) is hoppy, fruity and dry.

Hyde's are helping to recharge the local competitive spirit by introducing a series of seasonal ales. First came a refreshing, quaffable Summer Ale (3.2), very pale and dry hopped, then an autumnal dark ruby ale (4.2). There are also plans to re-introduce Fourex, a dark and powerful winter brew. Head brewer Allan Mackie said Hyde's intended to 'make it attractive for people to come to us rather than anyone else'.

But if Manchester today is noted for any particular beer beyond its own borders, it is Boddingtons Bitter. National giant Whitbread bought the city's oldest brewery in 1989 after the Boddington family's control had been watered down by outside share ownership. Having bought and closed numerous good breweries in the last quarter century simply to get at the accompanying tied pub estate, London-based Whitbread acquired Boddingtons Strangeways Brewery solely to add a classy ale brand to its own weakened portfolio.

Aided by its national pub estate and marketing muscle, Whitbread has turned Boddingtons Bitter (3.8) into a national brand, using broad appeal TV advertising. The Pilsener-coloured Bitter today has a more universally palatable malty, bitter-sweet taste than the once very bitter quenching beer made for men at the end of a mill shift. The Strangeways Brewery was founded in 1778 but the Boddingtons family involvement began only half a century later. Whitbread insists that Boddingtons Bitter will only ever be brewed in Manchester, even though production at Strangeways has tripled to 750,000 barrels a year since the Whitbread takeover. Perhaps more pertinent is how long will Boddington Bitter be with us? The Whitbread whim changes with the wind.

Other once great Manchester ales are now brewed elsewhere because of the accountants' curse: Chester's Mild at Leicester (for Whitbread); Wilson's Bitter at Mansfield, Notts (for Scottish-Courage); Oldham Bitter, at Burtonwood, Cheshire (for Whitbread). Under Whitbread's caring stewardship, Chester's Mild, once held in awe and known as 'Chester's Fighting Mild' has been moved twice across the Pennines and now to Leicester. Two mild beers – Boddingtons own dark style and Oldham Mild (both 3%) – were brewed at Strangeways until 1998 when they were phased out.

The disappearance of dozens of Manchester breweries this century was triggered by the oppressive 1904 Compensation Act which enabled licensing authorites to prune a district's pubs where they deemed numbers to be 'unnecessary'. This inevitably stiffened competition for beer outlets and therefore brewery mergers and takeovers. Peter Barnes, the local chairman of the Victorian Society and a pub preservation enthusiast, says that in addition hundreds of pubs were demolished in the last 40 years alone under slum clearances and road widening schemes. Fifty years ago within the city square mile alone there were 445 pubs; today there are 150.

Why then have so many nineteenth-century Manchester breweries survived? In the darkest days of the 1970s, as brewery closures intensified across the country and the survival of Britain's unique cask conditioned ale was threatened, Manchester remained a quiet oasis. Local competition kept beer prices at the lowest in the land, and they remain so. Adam Hyde points to a strong sense of commitment by the brewing families – helped, perhaps, by the gritty character for which Mancunians are noted. 'I think it is family involvement which keeps the companies independent. The key factor I think has been the willingness of the families to continue.'

But even as Manchester belatedly acknowledges its unique industrial past and seeks to preserve architectural remnants for posterity, there is no official recognition of the part played by beer and brewing in the life of the area. On the Salford boundary with Manchester, barely a mile from Boddingtons, stands the defunct Threlfalls Brewery. It is a classic piece of Victorian industrial architecture, built in 1893. It was shut down by Whitbread in 1989, and is now owned by a property development company. Despite being a Grade 2 listed building, the Victorian Society says the ex-brewery is suffering from 'unsympathetic changes'.

'This is a missed opportunity. It's the sort of building which should have been acquired by the National Trust,' Barnes believes. 'It is part of our cultural heritage.'

MALT AND HOPS

BY KEITH THOMAS

Take a good look at your pint. Ever noticed the colour? Swirl the glass and breathe in the heady aroma of hops. Take a mouthful and savour its taste. Is it a chemical concoction or a well crafted blend of flavours? Notice the body, the thickness and the mouthfeel? Relax and savour the aftertaste, particularly the bitterness and dryness. Notice how it dries the mouth, pulls in the cheeks and leaves you looking for another.

All of these characteristics come from the two major ingredients of beer – malt and hops. Both combine to provide the main flavours of beer. Take away hops and you have alcoholic, malt liquor; the sort of drink often experienced as bad homebrew. Brew with sugar instead and you have hoppy, alcoholic water, often exceedingly dry and harsh. Neither a drink to savour. Full blooded beer deserves flavours to enrich the palate, not dissolve it.

Colour is the first indication that beer is brewed from malt. Flavour is another. While drinking a beer look for fresh malt character, often experienced as caramel, biscuit or roast flavours. All of these come from malt, most of which will be pale in colour but, in some cases, copper-red or deep black. Malt is essential to beer. It provides the source of sugars for fermentation. It also provides colour, the foaming head and the rich flavours. If you are drinking your pint in the garden of a country pub look around for a field of barley. This is the beginning of your pint.

Barley varieties are many – traditional ones, such as Maris Otter, formed the backbone of many revered beers. Modern variants, such as Chariot and Target, were developed to match modern practices more exactly. Each variety can react differently in a mash giving a different character to a standard recipe. Chewing ripe malt grains gives an insight into their flavour. Look for a crisp bite and biscuit, Horlicks flavour with a slight bitterness as an aftertaste. Look for this in your next pint – often hiding behind the bitterness and hop character.

Malting barley is a cruel sport. Fresh grains are germinated, encouraged to grow roots and then roasted or stewed until burnt and dry. Without this treatment, however, starch could not be digested and the rich caramel and roast flavours associated with darker malts would not develop. So how did malt come to be used for beer? Possibly through barley being soaked by accident producing an alcoholic porridge as moulds and yeast grew on the starch. The early imbibers of this unexpected pleasure would have encountered more than a new variety of gruel and doubtless proceeded to replicate the effect as soon as sobriety returned. Such beers are still produced in many regions. Bantu beer is common in Africa, but is based on sorghum rather than barley. Cassava is used in South America with the distinction of being chewed and then spat into a bucket before fermentation. Digestive enzymes in saliva initiate the mashing making the product a distinctly sociable beer.

In contrast traditional malt production uses large vats to soak the malt before being spread over floors or piled deep in boxes to germinate. A quietness pervades maltings while barley germinates, disturbed only by the scraping of rakes to air the grains and untangle rootlets. Once growth is judged adequate grains are dried in a heated kiln, lightly for pale malt, more vigorously for coloured varieties. Taste a pint of bitter and then a dark mild. Note the bready and biscuit flavours in the bitter. Note the body in both. Body distinguishes beer from wine. Malt provides more than sugar for fermentation. In addition it provides complex sugars such as dextrins which survive fermentation to provide a thickness and physical character to beer. Taste wine against beer and note how dry and thin most wines are. Note how beer fills the mouth leaving body and fullness. Not that other grains cannot contribute to character. Corn, rice and wheat can all be used with barley malt in many beers to change character, dilute flavour or for simple economy. Additives can also contribute. Saccharine was prohibited from use in beer in 1888 since it elevates the palate impression of the malt. A beer may thus be brewed weaker but providing the same impression to the drinker and, of course, reduced revenue to the exchequer.

Hops are an altogether different ingredient in beer. Malt arrives by the ton and is carried by conveyor. Hops arrive in pockets and are dug out by the armful. They are the flowers of the hop plant and give beer pungent aromas from the lupulin glands in the base of their flower bracts. Agitate a glass of bitter and smell the fragrance. Taste the beer and note the bitterness. This also comes from hops and is typically the most impressionable and memorable character of beer.

Crush a hop flower between your palms and breathe in the pungent, floral aroma. Sticky resins are also released. These contain the alpha acids which are converted to bitterness compounds in the boil. A single dose of hops gives beer two of its major flavours – aroma and bitterness. The introduction of hops to Britain in the sixteenth century aroused fears that native beers would be adulterated. This was indeed true and the power of hops spelt a lingering death for native beers using only herbs and spices.

Different hop varieties contain variable levels of aroma and bitterness ingredients allowing numerous recipes to be formulated. Knowing the proportions used, however, cannot guarantee replication. The timing of hop addition is a further, and often critical, factor. Early, mid and late boil additions can create very different impressions as compounds react for different times. Few brewing books carry such secrets leaving the production of some of our best beers a subject of speculation.

Hops, even more than malt, have transient properties. Aroma rapidly vaporises when hops are exposed to air. Ingredients also oxidise leaving brown flowers with little flavour and reduced bitterness potential. Freshness is essential for most beers. Hops are heavily compressed into bales or powered into pellets to retain their character over the months after harvest. Some breweries use extracts produced from infusing hop flowers in chemical solvents. This provides a more consistent, but arguably more limited character to their products.

Are hops essential to beer? A number of brewers harbour residual desires to produce authentic medieval herb beers and may eventually revive a lost art. One major brewery, however, did address this issue directly in an unintentional experiment when an automatic hopping system refused to work. An entire five thousand gallons of beer was brewed, fermented and sold before the mistake appeared on the analysis sheet. The sum total of customer complaints were zero, doubtless indicating as much about the perception of the drinking public as about the brewery quality control.

In more distinctive beers, however, hops may account for more than 60 per cent of the perceived flavour. Strong India Pale Ales, for example, relied on an excessive hop charge to overcome the rigors of overseas travel to

India and beyond. Tasting such beers today causes the mouth to salivate so hard it can gum up with mucus. Not only were past drinkers hardy souls for their volume and alcohol intake but were also resistant to the extremes of human flavours.

Dark malts, particularly roast barley, were similarly used in stouts to produce a harshness and astringency typically associated with eating dried coffee by the spoonful. Today's stouts are a poor imitation of these robust beers, some of which were matured for a full year. Porters also used dark malts, but were probably a more even blend of ingredients, relying on brown, rather than black, malt. This intermediate malt was initially used in large proportions and provided a rounder and less distinct character, but one more suitable to balance with bitterness and fruitiness.

Porters and other beers are becoming increasingly popular as drinkers look for a greater variety on the bar. In fact the average number of cask ales produced in Britain's breweries has increased in recent times from 2.06 in 1979 to 4.33 in 1995. Each brand will have its own formulation of malt and hops to provide both major and subtle distinctions.

Whether these are perceivable by the drinker is another matter. Breweries commonly repeat stories where casks of ale are interchanged in the cellar during frantic serving periods, but with no consumer complaints. Knowledge of beer ingredients does not guarantee its enjoyment but does aid appreciation. And, after all, a moment of reverence is a small price to pay for the trials endured by the malt and hops and their contribution to the pint in your hand.

AN ECONOMIC SKETCH
of the brewing industry

BY IVOR CLISSOLD

British pubs and beer are in a radical and volatile market unknown since the early 19th century. And if the industry is not coping very well with this situation, they might reflect upon the plight of the Conservative Party, suddenly sidelined in politics following a defeat of a dimension similarly unparalleled since the Age of Reform. Their situations may not be unrelated.

An early fruit of Reform was Wellington's Beerhouse Act of 1830 (1 Will. IV, c 64), which enabled any householder assessed to the poor rate to open a beer-only pub by payment of two guineas to the local excise officer. Quoth the Duke:

> It was expedient for the better supplying of the public with beer in England to give greater facilities for the sale thereof than are at present afforded by licences to keepers of inns, alehouses and victualling-houses.

The number of licensed houses was not meeting demand all over the country. Why were there not more? Mr (later Lord) Brougham blamed JPs.

> In the first place, the justices have the privilege of granting or witholding licences. *As we all know*, it lies in the breast of two justices of the peace to give or refuse this important privilege. It is in their absolute power to give a licence to one of the most unfit persons possible, and it is in their power to refuse a licence to one of the

most fit persons possible. They may continue a licence to a person who has had it but twelve months, and who during that period has made his house a nuisance to the whole of the neighbourhood, or they may take away a licence from a house to which it has been attached for a century, and the enjoyment of which has not only been attended by no evil, but has been productive of great public benefit, and all this they do without even a shadow of control.

So why was a Whig MP slagging off JPs? Not just because the magisterial benches were predominantly Tories. The absolute power they possessed over pubs had corrupted them. They were reluctant to grant new licences except those given out of favouritism to strengthen their local influence. Of course, any publican involved in the Reform movement, or permitting his premises to be used for meetings was asking for disqualification, and the towns of England contained many radical publicans.

Before taxes on beer rose to today's absurd and market-depressing level, the principal cost was the grain. Let us recall the Corn Laws, which had no effect on music-hall comedians, but have helped many scholars to sleep since. England had traditionally produced sufficient grain for its population, but it was getting tight around 1800. Then the French wars cut foreign supplies and inferior land had to be cultivated, raising the price. The peace of 1815 was expected to see renewed imports and the inferior land fall out of use again. But the agricultural interests were not going to down-shift if they could avoid it, and a Corn Law was passed prohibiting imports. The government said they wanted to keep the poor land under the plough in case of another war. A likely story, thought others.

But the population grew so rapidly that supply was quite outstripped. Bread prices rose while the industrial revolution forced wages down. A compromise, a sliding scale was introduced in 1828, taxing imports 1s when the home price was 73s or more, rising to 3s when it stood at 64s, then increasing 1s with every 1s reduction. This did a bit of good, but not enough.

While the agricultural interest insisted upon protection, the industrialists favoured cheap imports, leading to cheap food and cheap wages. In 1838 the Anti-Corn Law League was formed. Peel tinkered with the sliding scale in 1841, with little improvement. The League got noisier, then the Irish potato famine of 1845 finally convinced Peel that cheap food had to come first. He turned round his Liberal cabinet and pushed the repeal Bill through the Commons under tremendous fire from Disraeli and Bentinck, both agricultural poodles. Wellington carried the Lords with him, the Bill passed in

June, grain prices fell and brewers felt smug.

The proliferation of beerhouses, many run part-time in cottage parlours, produced an increase in the number of common brewers (brewers for sale), who prior to this supplied mainly domestic trade. Now they had lots of business, but the pendulum had swung too far and there were too many beerhouses for the market to support. As tax was paid at source, the prime creditors of the straitened publicans were the common brewers, who often ended up owning estates of pubs in lieu of debts. The obvious advantage of controlling the outlets led to a pub collecting mania by the breweries, and soon the home-brewing pub was but a memory in most areas.

Thus Reform sowed the seeds of monopoly. After the pubs had settled down, innovation in beer styles halted. By the 1860s refrigeration offered up to a 40% production increase from year-round brewing; porter's challenger, IPA, was joined on the bar by its less demanding son, bitter.

If you'd have shared a quart of the new bitter with Karl Marx, he would have told you reform was again due. Capitalism was at the end of its era, and the proles would soon capture the means of brewing. But capitalism has another stage – monopoly capitalism – which saves it from completely eating itself by controlling competition and hence prices. It was assumed the brewing industry had reached this imago form in the early 1970s, when the Big Six dominated production and outlets, but this is now seen as a golden age of choice. In 1990, Secretary of State for Trade and Industry, Peter Lilley, gave conditional approval for the pubs-for-breweries swap between Courage and Grand Metropolitan, with the qualifier,

> I must consider each case on its merits, and the greater the degree of existing concentration in the industry, the more reluctant I will be to allow further increases in market share to take place by acquisition.

So government reluctance must have been amazingly grudging when they nodded Allied-Carlsberg through. The reluctance must have been monumental when the Courage-Scottish & Newcastle was approved. But approved they were, leaving four companies controlling 84 per cent of the UK beer market.

Such monopoly in private hands has not been seen since, perhaps, the East India Company, and such businesses turn out to behave just like state monopolies. Their staff turn into Stalinist apparatchiks, their awe of the system holding far more sway than anything the customers might say or want, and anxious to support the company line, without really knowing what it is. Dismal attempts to improve trade followed: not by improving their mediocre products, but dressing female staff as schoolgirls and holding vicars and tarts nights.

This must be the next and final stage of monopoly capitalism – decadence. How else can one explain:

- mediocre beers managed by brand managers who don't drink beer?
- pub vandalism by pub chain managers who don't use pubs?
- record sales of 'unprofitable' houses?
- alcopops?

The new reformist government's Margaret Beckett showed no signs of following her Lilley-livered predeccessor and courageously squashed the Bass attempt to take the Carlsberg-Tetley scalp, but this will not free up the market. Fortunately, their domination is incomplete and is now slipping. New enterprisers have arrived, and not before time, who can take a failed monopoly pub, give it more choice than it's ever had, restore the decor to sanity, remove the electronical gismos and appreciate a silence only broken by the hubbub of conversation and the jingle of the tills. Such operators are not just corporate companies like Wetherspoons, who, it seems, have the effrontery to change an aircraft hangar into a record-busting boozer, but small, local businessmen who can see where the big boys are going wrong, and proceed to prove it by buying one of their no-hope pubs and making it thrive.

Equally exciting has been the boom in cottage brewing. Encouraged by the guest beer law, hundreds of one and two person craft breweries have opened, many not knowing a business plan from a bankruptcy petition, but soon finding out. It is to be hoped that this craze for opening breweries settles down, as a number of excellent plants have already closed due to market glut.

And while all this has been going on the independent, family breweries have been plodding away, mostly delivering high class beers, and still earning enough to pay their subs to the county set. Like the smaller operators, they are closer to their customers and tend to respond to their requirements. This often means doing nothing, rather than trying to tell the public what they think the public want. Doing nothing is seen as a weakness by the monopolists: in fact it can be a great strength.

But swapping pub ownership from mega-operator to big independent pub chain does not always improve beer choice. Pub chains are able to offer cheap beer because they buy it cheaply in bulk, and that has something to do with it being brewed cheaply in bulk. Unfortunately, that is also how it tastes, and it is probably the same beer as was on sale during the previous regime.

If all the new pub chains achieve is to drive the monopolies out of pub operations and into cut-throat mega-brewing, we shall not be much further forward. Already some independent breweries have taken the route of quitting brewing altogether to concentrate upon managing their pub estates. Many of these pubs will end up selling the monopolists' cheap beer.

Publicans make pubs in their own image, and adjust decor, music, etc., to their own liking, in the sure conviction the world will approve. The Bass/Allied/Scottish Courage/Whitbread quadropoly have taken identical routes and cluttered out their pubs with twenty-something managers, who create pubs for twenty-somethings. Even if the managers do nothing, the offices full of pub designers will never declare themselves redundant and consequently perpetuate endless pub wrecking programmes. When they have wrecked all the pubs, they simply start again. They may even restore them to something like the original, but this is rare. The usual rule is to backdate a pub by one period: any post WW2 house, is made Edwardian, Edwardian pubs are made Victorian, Victorian is made Georgian, and, dodgy on history, Georgian becomes mediaeval. Or screw a bicycle and a few groceries to the walls and call it Irish.

Unsurprisingly, thousands of customers over thirty have stopped going out for a drink. They do not need a bouncer on the door to tell them they do not fit. So many of the monopolists' pubs have had their customer balance upset in this way, losing the cross-sectional benefits that community pubs bring, not to mention the moderating influence of adult presence upon the young. With dark decor and the loud music forcing shouting matches, no wonder aggression is so common.

Meanwhile the monopolists continue to squabble and throw their bloated weight about over shares of an ever-crumbling cake. The independents, on the other hand, are not too bothered. They have got a new cake, and it is getting bigger, as people arrive who have not used pubs for years, if ever.

It is prehaps too early to assess the full effects of Mrs Beckett's decision, but already Allied Domecq have announced a refurbishment programme that may go some way towards humanising some of the filling stations that pass off as pubs. Reform is again in the air. Perhaps it is an idea whose time has come.

Ivor Clissold died in October 1997 and his article has been left as written apart from style editing.

THE FALL AND RISE
of the micro-breweries

BY ALISTAIR HOOK

The fall and rise of micro-brewing charts the story of the struggle between the technology and the art of brewing. In so doing it follows a change in the relationship that humanity has had with the fruits of its labour.

Beer in Babylon
The term micro-brewing is a contemporary name for the production of beer on a small scale. The small scale production of beer has a history as long as civilisation itself. It spans the ages and with it forms a common thread through cultural development of mankind. The inextricable link between primordial societies and the cultivation of cereal, and the social transition from a hunter-gatherer to communal dweller, provided the foundations for the world we live in and the breweries we brew in.

Some historians have gone as far as to say that the establishment of an Ancient Egyptian civilisation was catalysed by the need to produce beer. Even today however some 70% of mans nutritional intake is made up of starch, and it was probably this fact alone that was the key motivation for the early settlers of Mesopotamia.

Dr E Huber in his 1926 publication *Beer, Brewing and the Birth of Mankind* gave an insight into early domestic brewing methods. Barley it was said was put in earthenware vessels and placed in the ground until germination began. It was then crushed and made into dough, baked and broken up into biscuits. This biscuits or cakes could be easily transported and when combined with water at a convenient oasis fermentation could take place. This acid beer was called 'Boozah'. It would have been easy to imagine the production of bread, from the indigenous crop emmer, a type of wheat unsuitable for brewing, alongside the daily 'chore' of beer making.

Ancient micro-brewers

The early history of brewing, articulated more fully elsewhere in this book, charts, by definition, the history of small brewing. Modern history and the development of an 'industrialised society' has commercialised the production of beer, the breweries have grown in size and the small brewery has dwindled in number. The spirit of micro-brewing however is the same today as it was in ancient times. It represents the closest link between humans and their maker, the soil, the seasons and his cardinal nature. The popularity of micro-breweries in our 'post industrial' society shows how the essential art of brewing has not been lost, and how, despite seismic changes in human lifestyles, certain fundamentals remain the same.

The medieval brewhouse

The unchanged nature of small brewing practice over the ages is easily described using a simple historical comparison. Today, a micro-brewery, producing 20 barrels of beer a week, forming part of a pub or standing alone in an industrial unit would typically be composed of the following:- mill for the cracking of the malt: hot liquor tank and a cold liquor tank, for brewing with and chilling with respectively: mash tun for the mixing of malted barley and hot water to affect the extraction of malt sugars from the barley husk: brewing copper for boiling the sweet wort with the hops: plate and frame heat exchanger for the cooling of boiled hopped wort: yeast tub for the collection and storage of yeast: number of fermenting tuns or vessels for the conversion of the sugars to alcohol: large quantity of casks for the disbursement of beer to trade: number of pumps, hoses and buckets. The all-in price, in second hand condition might come to £10,000 at today's prices.

A Listing in a will left to a brewer Laurence Long, in the parish of St Martin's, Ludgate, in 1335 ran as follows: 'Two leaden vessels; one leaden cistern; one leaden tap trough; one old chest; one mash vat, value 18d; one fining vat, valued 6d; one tresel for barrels, valued 12d; three sets of hand-mills, valued 4s; one piece of lead, valued 2d; one tun and one half tun, valued 8d; one ale vat, valued 18d; five keme-lynes, valued 10d; one clensingbuche, valued 10d. ; also one alegiste, valued 2d.'.

The growth of commercial breweries

Micro-brewing was historically speaking the only form of brewing. It was conducted by ale-wives in the house, or kitchen, and formed just another task along with the baking of bread and cooking of meals. The evolution of brewing from the kitchen to the public house was a small step in itself but would have heralded the first shifts from a cottage industry to more centralised forms of production. In London in 1319 almost 1300 breweries existed, either attached to or a part of the public house. Home or domestic breweries were similarly prolific in rural areas. Just as the growth of towns acted as the prelude to industrialisation, so it also led to the gradual decline in the number of breweries per head of population. In the towns, house breweries became pub breweries and pub breweries became small independent breweries.

The number of breweries in the city of London had fallen to three hundred by 1419, although each would have remained small and would supply one, two or a number of alehouses in the locality. The gradual increase in town populations led to proportional closures of breweries and the ones that remained increased production accordingly. Although the sixteenth and seventeenth centuries saw a continuation of this trend it was the advent of the industrial revolution that heralded the end of pub and house brewing in the cities. The eighteenth century gave birth to steam, coke, pumps, hydrometers, thermometers, and mechanical devices such as grain conveyors and mixers. These innovations, combined with the concentration and increases in populations in cities and towns contributed to the demise of the small brewer.

The improvement in transport systems was another key to the subsequent development of the commercial brewery. Economies of scale in large population centres also gave plenty of profit incentive to the wealthy to invest in larger breweries. The late nineteenth century saw the early days of venture capitalism and were best highlighted by the growth of Guinness in Dublin, Bass in Burton and Allsopps of London. With the establishment of large companies, the real power of 'brands' began to take a hold. Marketing techniques took on a new dimension. The strength of the Guinness and Bass brands are unparalleled to this day.

Despite much progress, technology in the brewery remained relatively simple up until the end of the nineteenth century. Fuelled by new capital however, the brewery was well set to begin the physical transition to the massive beer factories that produce 90 per cent of the world's beer today.

Winners and losers

The demise of micro-brewery then ran in parallel with the growth of the industrial society and the technological achievements that made it possible. The history of brewing in Britain is a story of development and change from a cottage industry to a multi billion pound commercial business. The rapid application of technology to the brewing industry itself over the past two hundred years has combined with the changes in basic commercial practice and marketing to transform the industry beyond recognition. As rationalisation began in the early days of the industrial revolution, as markets evolved overseas, as demand for beer necessitated more efficient practice, so the share of the market belonging to the micro brewer contracted to a point of insignificance. Brewery expansions and take-overs became the norm and rationalisation led to small numbers of prolific producers of beer.

Implications of industrialisation

The gradual disappearance of brewing within communities meant that the common appreciation and understanding of beer had been lost. The local brewer was once the focal point of this understanding, his very presence was part of the educational process that yielded greater enjoyment and appreciation of his product. Beer lost its presence in folklore and the art of brewing had been subordinated by technology, the growth fuel of commerce.

Beer has become a mass produced commodity. It has a utility, a function, and in consequence is no longer an object of sensual pleasure. Current debate on the well-being of the brewing industry seldom refers to the cultural significance of beer. It might refer obliquely to educating the public, or to publicity drives, but seldom does it question the very structure of the industry or the relationship that exists between brewer and beer drinker. The cultural status of beer began to decline when breweries began to close.

The rise of the new brewers

Despite the commercial decline of the small breweries, recent figures for the brewing industry world-wide have in shown that dramatic reversals of this trend have been taking place in the last thirty years. These increases have been most notable in the USA and UK where growth has been almost exponential since 1990. In 1995 approximately 200 micros opened up in the USA and 90 in the UK.

The UK currently has 280 micros. A new brewery is opening every week and it is quite possible that double the current number will exist early in the new millennium. The number of small breweries in the early 1970s could be counted on one hand. Forty more were to open by 1980 and a further 168 by 1990.

More than 1,000 small breweries now exist in the USA. This compares with none in 1975, 30 in 1985 and 211 in 1990. Failure rates are currently standing at one in seven. The staggering growth in the size of these breweries have lead to a new classification entitled 'speciality regional'. These breweries produce over 15,000 barrels of beer a year and in 1993 numbered nine. Micro-brewed beer now represents 2$^1/_2$ per cent of national production and in the state of Oregon it has reached 10 per cent. The 1995 Great American Beer Festival played host to 335 micro-breweries offering a total of 1,345 different beers.

The interest that the micro-breweries are generating amongst the press, media and public is symptomatic of a time where disillusionment with lifestyles and a reaction towards technology is commonplace. The diversity, choice and zest that micro-breweries, their brewers, and their beers bring to a world of corporate blandness and homogeneity have proved extremely popular. It must be recognised that high unit costs and product inconsistencies are on the other hand the weaknesses that have worked against the micro-brewery. Somewhere in between however the consumer has helped to create a niche that is the micro-brewers' appreciative market.

Micro-brewing is not an industry, it is a lifestyle. It echoes time honoured values of communication and common appreciation between the brewer and the beer drinker. It generates and adds quality to the lives of all those involved and in many ways replaces all that has been lost as a result of the downsides of technological development.

A golden age awaits
The age of considered consumption, where the consumer expresses new found economic freedom by demanding choice and variety, by exercising his right to what he wants, heralds the new dawn of the micro-brewer. The fruits of technological and economic revolutions and developments have generated vast populations with disposable income but restricted choice. The compromises that mankind has made to his artistic development has yielded a wealth and with it a reappraisal of values. Rationalisation and economic progress increases standards of living but can work against the quality of life. It works against choice, variety, authenticity and quality.

The difference between the micro-brewery and the brewery is difficult to comprehend, but the experience of the last eight thousand years give one possible insight. Albert Einstein remarked in 1918 that only intuition, resting on a sympathetic understanding of experience can find the harmonies necessary in life to balance the utility and aesthetical content of science and art respectively. Experience was scientific understanding, art was the intuition. The micro-brewery of 1990s marries the fundamentals of brewing science with the romantic expression of the culinary arts. It uses the basic principles of thermodynamics, biochemistry and micro-biology to achieve an intelligible understanding of the brewing process. Sound science means consistency is assured and the brewer can then go about expressing his art, in a way that the consumer is once again beginning to appreciate and enjoy

INDEPENDENT BREWERS

BY MICHAEL HARDMAN

Mention Cockermouth to any knowledgeable beer drinker and it's a pound to a pinch of yeast that you won't get a lecture on Wordsworth's birthplace. Similarly, you can be safely insured against a diatribe on rowing if you slip Henley-on-Thames into the conversation. Instead of Lakeland poets and strapping young men in striped blazers, the thoughts of our learned lounge lizard will immediately turn to Jennings Brothers and Brakspears, two of the 50 or so long-established independent family breweries dotted around Britain, still producing traditional ales as they have done for centuries.

These companies, tantalisingly called Hydes Anvil and Hook Norton or workaday Joseph Holt or George Gale, between them own around 10,000 pubs and produce 500 brands of beer, more than half of them real ales, Britain's unique and often undervalued form of draught beer. They employ well over 10,000 people directly, perhaps an additional 75,000 in their pubs, and create work for countless thousands more in allied industries such as farming, transport and glass-making. Most important of all, these brewing companies, from Timothy Taylor of Keighley, on the edge of the Yorkshire Dales, to St Austell in deepest Cornwall, quench the thirsts of millions of discerning British beer-drinkers, as well as providing a vast variety of premises where people can drink, eat, meet, play games and enjoy informal banking facilities when in need of a tenner on a Sunday evening.

All very cosy, you might think, as you run your index finger down the list, from Adnams of Southwold, in remote Suffolk, to Young's of

Wandsworth in bustling London. But beware. Our independent brewers have been reduced from 6,000 in number at the beginning of the 20th century to just over 50 at the start of the 21st, if you don't count the new wave of micro-brewers and pubs that produce their own beer. What's more, the very existence of the few that remain is seriously threatened.

Not content with allowing widely differing and unfair rates of excise duty to apply in what is now supposed to be a truly common market – a situation that puts British brewers at a distinct disadvantage in competition with French brewers, for instance – the European Commission has been threatening, on and off for years, to review what it quaintly calls a block exemption. The exemption in question frees all European brewers from the effects of Article 85 of the Treaty of Rome, which prohibits agreements deemed likely to fetter free competition.

The heart of the problem is the centuries-old system of brewers owning pubs and letting them to self-employed tenant publicans, who are required to buy all, or most, of their beer from the owner-brewers. This is known as the brewers' tie and although practised in one form or another in Continental Europe and, indeed, throughout the world, is much more prevalent and deep-rooted in Britain than anywhere else. Brewers also own a different kind of tied pub – the managed house, where an employee of the brewery is the publican and is paid a salary – but the European Commission is proposing no action to change this state of affairs. Supporters of the tie – drinkers, publicans, politicians and brewers alike – argue that it is essential to the future health of Britain's independent brewing companies and that it has preserved the wide choice of beer styles and brands available within these shores. They point to countries that have abolished the tie more or less completely, such as the United States, Canada and Australia, which now find themselves dominated by a handful of brewing companies providing a woefully limited choice of unimaginative beers.

The independent brewers have been leading the fight to maintain the tie and have won a number of reprieves from the European Commission. But the long-term threat to the tie remains just below the surface, ready to bubble up at any time the Commission takes a fancy. Thirty-six family brewers banded together in 1993 as the Independent Family Brewers of Britain, or IFBB, with this issue uppermost in their minds, though they have also been heard vociferously campaigning for harmonisation of excise duty and other causes, notably support for real ale. The IFBB membership rose to 38 just after its formation but has now slipped to 34 after the demise of four breweries in the past few years. Nevertheless, the IFBB is still a powerful force.

Its members produced more than 500 million pints of beer, more than 70 per cent of it real ale, in the year up to June 1999. The case to preserve the tie is based on the argument that without a secure local market, local breweries will be forced to cut down on the number of beers they make or possibly find it is more economical to stop brewing altogether, a decision already taken by a small number of companies that still own pubs but buy their beer from other brewers.

The IFBB are wholeheartedly supported by CAMRA, the Campaign for Real Ale, which broadly gives its backing to independent brewers but sometimes doesn't see eye to eye with individual companies. CAMRA says: 'The tied house system gives the customer a wide choice of locally brewed, distinctive beers at reasonable prices. Abolition of the tie would have a catastrophic effect on customer choice. Far from increasing competition, it would mean fewer beers and higher prices.'

The IFBB chairman, Anthony Fuller, who is also chairman of Fuller's Brewery in London, writes in the IFBB's 1999 annual report:

'The brewing and pub retailing industry has undergone another year of radical change with brewery closures, mergers and take-overs dominating the headlines. There are now only 75 breweries left in the UK (excluding micros)... this continued haemorrhaging represents a serious threat to the future of the small and medium-sized family-owned brewers in the UK. The government has not listened to the arguments on the problems caused by the massive and largely illegal importation of cheap foreign beers. Customs officers are overwhelmed by the daily 1.5 million pints of beer coming into the UK from the Continent and UK brewers are still having to compete on an unfair playing field.'

The problems caused and threats posed by unequal rates of duty are much greater than most people realise. If you multiply Anthony Fuller's 1.5 million pints a day by the number of days in a year, you get 547,500,000 pints a year, a shade less than the entire annual output of the 36 IFBB members put together. That should send a shudder down the spine of every beer drinker in the land.

In spite of the loss of so many breweries over the decades, Britain still produces one of the widest varieties of beer brands and beer styles in the world. The average British pub has more beers on offer – not to mention wines, spirits and soft drinks – than bars anywhere else. To preserve this state of affairs, and particularly to safeguard traditional cask-conditioned or real ale, measures must be taken urgently to help the independent brewers to survive. As the IFBB's report says: 'Cask-conditioned beer is integral to

INDEPENDENT BREWERS

Britain's brewing heritage. Because the secondary fermentation takes place in the cellar of the pub, it needs care and expertise to ensure that each pint is served in perfect condition. National brewers have largely withdrawn from cask ale and are no longer supporting cask ales with the vital national advertising campaigns which underpin consumption. Cask ale now represents a mere 10.9 per cent of the beer market, a drop of 17 per cent in four years. The Family Brewers passionately believe real ale has a future. There is demand for good quality cask-conditioned beers and our Family Brewers will continue to offer a superb range of quality beers in all our pubs. This may well prove the difference between Family Brewers and others; the care, pride and investment put into cask ales to protect choice and diversity.'

And finally, a personal, and admittedly subjective, selection of Britain's best beers includes 14 produced by the established independents:

Bateman's XB (3.8 per cent alcohol by volume): a lovely bitter beer from Wainfleet in south Lincolnshire. The brewery, which is built round an old windmill, was saved after a family dispute in the 1980s.

Batham's Best Bitter (4.3 per cent): one of the palest real ales in the country and one of the most distinctive. Produced at a tiny brewery behind the Vine (or the Bull and Bladder, as the locals call it) at Brierley Hill in the West Midlands.

Brain's Bitter (4.2 per cent): a delightfully dry beer, brewed in Cardiff and locally known as Light to distinguish it from the stronger SA best bitter.

Brakspear's Bitter (3.4 per cent): proof that beer doesn't need to be strong to have masses of flavour, mainly from hops in this case. Made in Henley-on-Thames by brewers not oarsmen.

Fuller's ESB (5.5 per cent): a thick and fruity bitter from Chiswick in west London, best reserved for the last pint (or two) of a session.

Gale's Prize Old Ale (9.0 per cent): real ale in a bottle, from Horndean, in the Hampshire countryside north of Portsmouth. Dark, fruity, powerful and memorable.

Holt's Bitter (4.0 per cent): one of the last remaining local beers from Manchester, which still boasts Britain's heaviest concentration of breweries despite recent closures and mergers. Holt's Bitter is distinctive in the extreme and so much the better for it.

Jennings Bitter (3.5 per cent): another highly distinctive beer, this time from Cockermouth in the Lake District. A splendid balance of malt and hops.

McMullen's Original AK (3.7 per cent): a light mild when I first came across it 20-odd years ago, but now described by the brewery in Hertford as a bitter, without having changed its distinctive, dry taste.

Palmer's Best Bitter (4.2 per cent): the best of the West Country beers, from Britain's only thatched brewery, in Bridport, Dorset. Another successful balance of malt and hops.

Robinson's Old Stockport Bitter (3.5 per cent): apart from the new name, which replaced plain, old-fashioned Bitter a year or two back, everything is good about this beautifully refreshing ale from Stockport, particularly its vice-like grip on the drinker's inability to refuse another.

Thwaites's Bitter (3.6 per cent): one of the best balanced beers in Britain, brewed in Blackburn, which was until relatively recently a major brewing centre.

Timothy Taylor's Landlord (4.3 per cent): a beautiful beer, full of fruit and hops. The best thing to come out of Yorkshire since Fred Trueman and Jim Laker.

Young's Bitter (3.7 per cent): one of Britain's great ales. I have been enjoying the delights of this bitterest of bitters for many, many years and hope to do so until I can sup no more.

LOUIS PASTEUR
And the brewing industry

BY NICHOLAS REDMAN

Louis Pasteur spent just six years looking at the problems of beer diseases, fermentation and yeasts, but the results of his efforts had a dramatic and lasting effect on the industry.

Pasteur had already carried out studies in the fields of lactic and alcoholic fermentation and the manufacture of vinegar in the 1850s. In 1863 he began to study the diseases of wine which caused the industry immense commercial losses. His results were published in 1866 in *Études sur le vin*.

In spring 1871 Pasteur set off with his family from his home in Arbois in the Jura intending to continue his researches on silkworm disease in the laboratory of his friend, Professor Emile Duclaux, at the Faculty of Sciences at Clermont-Ferrand in Pûy-de-Dôme.

But while there he became interested in the problems of beer production and started work at 'the only brewery in the neighbourhood of Clermont', M. Kühn's establishment at Chamalières. He was warmly welcomed by the brewer who gave him every support and assistance.

Pasteur's patriotic pride had been deeply wounded by France's humiliating defeat in 1870-71 at the hands of the Prussians and it was with thoughts of revenge that he now undertook this work. He reasoned that if he could apply scientific principles to the manufacture of French beer and improve its quality it might be possible to oust the Germans, the superiority of whose beers he acknowledged, from their markets.

So much was this a factor in his work at Chamalières that when he applied in June to the Clermont authorities for a patent for his 'new method of brewing', he specified that all beer brewed using his method should be called 'Bières de la Revanche Nationale' (Beers of the National Revenge).

Kühn's Brewery no longer stands, but a plaque on the site carries the following momentous inscription: 'En ce lieu s'élevait la Brasserie Kühn où l'illustre Pasteur fit au cours de l'année 1871, des recherches sur les fermentations.'

By August Pasteur realised that to progress with his investigations he needed to work at a larger brewery than Kühn's. He decided to come to London to see 'one of those English Breweries which produce more than 100,000 hectolitres of beer a year'.

He arrived in London in September 1871. In the course of the next two weeks he visited several concerns. 'Every morning he left the Grosvenor Hotel in Victoria where he was staying, to go to the various breweries which he was now privileged to see in their smallest details,' his biographer Vallery-Radot writes. The name of only one of these breweries is known – Whitbread's

Several English breweries both in London and Burton were already using microscopes at this date, but Whitbread's was not one of them.

On his arrival at Chiswell Street Pasteur asked for a little of the yeast of the porter which was flowing into the trough from the cask. He examined it with the microscope he had brought with him and soon recognised 'a noxious ferment which he drew on a piece of paper, remarking: 'This porter must leave much to be desired,' to the astonished managers who had not expected this sudden criticism.'

'He added that surely the defect must have been betrayed by a bad taste, perhaps already complained of by some customers. The managers admitted that only that morning they had been forced to get fresh yeast from another brewery.'

Pasteur next examined the yeast of the pale ale then being brewed and again found contamination. Gradually samples of every kind of beer on the premises were brought to Pasteur and put under the microscope.

As Pasteur worked on at Chiswell Street the enormous importance of what he was saying dawned on the brewery managers. Whitbread, like many other brewers, sustained heavy losses from unpredictable changes in their beers, averaging around 20 per cent of total production.

They lost no time in buying a microscope and when Pasteur returned for a second visit a week later he was able to use it. Whitbread's scientific tradition may be said to date from Pasteur's visit, and the microscope, a fine binocular one by Beck, remains a prized souvenir of the occasion.

Pasteur returned to France and during the next four years continued his researches, with his team of assistants, working at a pilot brewery he established at the École Normale in Paris where various beers were carefully examined. Between 1873 and 1875 much work was done at the Tourtel brothers' large brewery at Tantonville, near Nancy.

In 1876 Pasteur published his *Études sur la bière*, translated into English three years later by Faulkner and Robb and published as *Studies on Fermentation*.

The main portion of the book is devoted to Pasteur's contention that every fermentation and every putrefaction is brought about by micro organisms. 'Fermentation is a result of life without air.' The book is really more a classic of medical literature: only two chapters are directed specifically at the practical problem of brewing. Pasteur did not like beer very much himself and took but a slight interest in the question of its flavour and taste. What mattered to him was whether it was sound and free from contamination.

One subject *Études sur la bière* does not deal with in detail is pasteurisation. His ideas on this had in fact emerged several years earlier during his studies on wine. Although primarily intended for wine growers the idea had been rapidly taken up by German and Austrian bottled beer producers from the mid 1860s. Pasteurisation of beers on the continent became widespread. In England, however, there was less interest. Top-fermented beers 'suffered in flavour and became turbid on keeping'.

In 1884 Pasteur visited Edinburgh to attend the tercentenary of the university. As the guest of Henry Johnstone Younger he went to the Abbey and Holyrood Breweries, spent some time in the laboratories and, having examined the yeast under the microscope, pronounced it 'pure', to the delight of his hosts.

The same year he also went to Copenhagen and had a chance to see for himself Jacobsen's magnificent Carlsberg brewery and the laboratory, inspired by Pasteur, which had become a leading centre of biochemical research. Jacobsen was an ardent admirer of Pasteur. He commissioned a bust by Dubois and a painting by Bonnat and, in 1892, organised a commemorative medal to mark his 70th birthday.

Pasteur's discoveries were part of a long process taking the industry from the days when, as the *Brewers' Journal* put it, 'our sole knowledge rested on blind empiricism or rule of thumb'. The mysteries of yeast and fermentation had engaged the attentions of many since Van Leeuwenhoek made his drawings of yeast cells in 1680, and men like Lavoisier and Gay-

Lussac, for example. In the 1830s Schwann, Cagniard-Latour and Kutzing separately, but almost simultaneously, demonstrated that yeast is a living organism.

Pasteur laid down three great principles:

- Every alteration either of the wort or of the beer itself depends on the development of micro-organisms which are ferments of disease.
- These germs of ferment are brought by air, by the ingredients, or by the apparatus used in breweries.
- Whenever beer contains no living germs it is unalterable.

Not every one agreed, notably Justus Liebig in Germany whose view that the process of fermentation was associated with decomposition, rather than life, still influenced the attitude of many. The Liebig-Pasteur controversy continued for several years.

Pasteur's work was, of course, not the end of the matter. Research continued, most notably at the Carlsberg laboratory where the great Emil Christian Hansen 'took up Pasteur's work and carried it to lengths then hardly dreamed of', developing methods of pure cultivation by which single cells were isolated and the characteristic pure races determined, which became the basis of all further advances in the study of micro-organisms.

It could be argued that the revolution in brewing chemistry triggered by Pasteur and his successors did not lead to a revolution in brewing practice, although it is true that an 'enlightened few', which included Whitbread's, benefited enormously from a proper appreciation and understanding of Pasteur's laboratory results. However in this country there remained a hostility to the march of brewing science and an ignorance of Pasteur's work. The organisers of the fund raising money to establish the Pasteur Institute in Paris were shocked to be told by brewers that 'they had heard of Pasteur's experiments on dogs, but never knew he had anything to do with beer. When it was put to these gentlemen that he had possibly saved the brewers of this country upwards of a million pounds sterling we were met by a blank look of astonishment mingled with doubt'. It is not surprising that in the 1890s there were still many breweries that did not have a microscope.

Overall, however, there is no doubt that Pasteur's efforts meant, as Richard Wilson puts it, 'The dark ages of empiricism were at an end. After decades of false and incomplete trails Pasteur explained the fermentation process precisely in terms of the life cycle of yeast.' We may, I think, divide the development of brewing science into two categories: Before Pasteur, and After Pasteur.

LOUIS PASTEUR AND THE BREWING INDUSTRY

On Pasteur's death in 1895 one newspaper wrote: 'When the century comes to an end and those who have laboured in the service of progress and of science are passed in review, Pasteur's will be the name always mentioned with honour by the grateful brewer.'

On 28th September 1995, the exact centenary of Pasteur's death, the British Guild of Beer Writers organised a special seminar at Whitbread's in Chiswell Street, London, to celebrate his achievements. A number of speakers looked at Pasteur's general contribution to the brewing industry, the more specifically technical side of his work, and his achievements in other fields.

There was also a display of Pasteur material, including the famous microscope bought by Whitbread in 1871. Among the beers on offer was one brewed especially for the occasion by a Guild member. It was called 'Bière de la Revanche Nationale' in acknowledgement of the events that led directly to Pasteur's work on beer.

In a separate tribute Whitbread issued a special edition of 'Louis Pasteur Ale', limited to just 100 bottles, to the memory of the man whose work 'inaugurated a new era in the history of beer brewing'. The bottles were distributed to key figures in the industry, and to those with Pasteur connections.

On 9th September 1996 Whitbread marked the exact 125th anniversary of Pasteur's historic 1871 visit to their brewery when the Secretary of State for National Heritage, Virginia Bottomley, unveiled a plaque in front of a distinguished audience of representatives from the Royal Society, the Royal Society of Chemistry, the French Embassy, the Pasteur Institute in Paris, the Academy of Sciences in Paris, and the great-niece of Louis Pasteur.

BASS
A humorous view

BY MAURICE LOVETT

Beer has always attracted the attention of writers and artists. Such luminaries as A E Houseman, Chaucer, Shakespeare, Brendan Behan, Dylan Thomas and even the apostle of common sense, Samuel Johnson, were enthusiasts for beer. Johnson also ran a brewery for a time, after the death of his patron's husband, Henry Thrale. It was this task that led Johnson to coin the phrase 'the potentiality of growing rich beyond the dreams of avarice' when he sold the brewery.

But my favourite is W C Fields, who raised the art of drinking to new heights with such witticisms as 'who stole the cork from my lunch' and 'we lived for days on nothing but food and water'. Oddly, it was the period between 1850 and 1950 that mined the richest vein of beery literature. Perhaps it is due to the advent of the nanny society, which preaches that everything pleasant is bad for you, that wit and beer went into a decline – a problem that is thankfully now being rectified by the Guild.

Although many beers have appeared in literature, drawings and paintings, the one that achieved immortality was Bass.

Perhaps this is not surprising. Bass was a famously successful international beer long before the mineral water swigging lads in red braces who call themselves 'brand managers' reinvented the concept and claimed it as their own. The Bass Red Triangle trademark is the world's oldest and Bass in bottle was available everywhere where the sun never sets (and a few other places as well). From the Tea House of the Moon Temple on Mount Maya in Japan to the dining cars of the Union Pacific Railroad in the USA, you could get a bottle of Bass.

As a result, its merits were lauded in the pages of every improbable publication you can name and the bottle of Bass Ale was an essential prop for painters everywhere. It also had the advantage that once you had painted it, you could drink it. Many of these early literary references paid tribute to Bass's capabilities for curing everything from kidney stones to impotence and probably cleaning the curtains, shampooing the carpet and reupholstering the three piece suite at the same time. In today's cotton-wool wrapped society, such enthusiasm would be condemned out of hand and the Thought Police, the Cook Report and the BBC Watchdog team would be on the doorstep in double quick time, but one hundred and fifty years ago, people were expected to have a mind of their own.

Which is why in *John Bull* in 1840, a Dr Prout roundly condemned common ale and recommended Bass for weakly persons. *Pearson's Weekly*, another respected and eminently sober publication, recommended Bass as a cure for... well, just listen to this: 'An old friend of mine, Colonel Worsley CB, when in India, had a very dangerous attack of dysentery and was given up by the doctors. When dying as it was thought, he begged his man in a faint whisper to get him some Bass and as it was thought his case was hopeless he was humoured. He then drank pint after pint and began to get better as soon as his yearning was satisfied much to the astonishment of his doctors and brother officers.'

And I can understand their astonishment, given the normal effects of Bass on the human plumbing system: they say that Burton upon Trent was the only town in Britain where Bass was recommended by local doctors as the only laxative worth considering.

Nineteenth-century literature mines a rich vein of most bizarre claims for Bass. *The Times* has a recommendation from a Dr Mapother for Bass as a cure for gout. The *Civil Service Gazette* of 1890 lists Burton's finest as a cure for Civil Service hangovers: 'it is something reviving when one is a little out of sorts, something one can fly to with a distinct relish when the morning brings an awakening to overnight indiscretions'. In the book *Younghusband up the Khyber* (honestly, that's the real title) a quart bottle of Bass is used as a weapon to dispose of a poisonous snake. In *The Follies of Edward VII* a book which could well have been fiction, its quotes are so improbable, there is an account of how the Prince of Wales was struck down with typhoid. Whilst dangerously ill – so ill that his wife Alexandra had to be barred from the sick room because in his fever he was reciting the not inconsiderable list of his lady friends – he was fed with quantities of

Bass and as a result, made a miraculous recovery.

Bass has also made regular appearances in plays, novels and even poems. We all know about its major role in *The Entertainer*, although given the drink soaked state of the main character, Archie Rice, I'm not sure if it's a recommendation for regular imbibing. In Rudyard Kipling's poem, *The Jacket*, dedicated to the Royal Horse Artillery, there is every soldiers top priority: 'save the beer first'. It reads:

> Then we trotted gentle not to break the bloomin' glass,
> Though the Arabites 'ad all their ranges marked;
> But we dursn't 'ardly gallop, for the beer was bottled Bass,
> An' we'd dreamed of it since we was disembarked.

But certainly the best known reference of all is in Dorothy L Sayers' classic mystery, *The Nine Tailors*, where Bass helps Lord Peter Wimsey to solve a murder. After much praise for the beer, he quaffs a quart bottle in the village local, the Red Cow, before persuading the landlord, the admirable Mr Donnington, to supply him with a list of customers, which puts him on to the trail of the culprit.

In art, the fame of the Bass red triangle trade mark and the beer it advertised led to it appearing in pictures, prints, drawings, book illustrations, sculptures, collages and constructions.

It's surprising how many times the ubiquitous bottle appears in book illustrations. It's in Ronald Searle's Penguin edition of his *Dear Diary*; in Arthur Rackham's illustrations for an early edition of the *Wind in the Willows*, as Ratty appears from a cupboard with four bottles of Bass under his arm; Quentin Blake's illustration for Roald Dahl's *The Twits* as Mr Twit sits with six bottles of Bass in front of him; and even in an illustration by Sir Max Beerbohm for the book *Rossetti and his Circle*.

The most famous – and most valuable – painting that includes a bottle of Bass is Manet's *Bar at the Folies Bergeres*, now in the Courtald Collection. I'm reliably informed that if it ever came up for sale, you wouldn't get a lot of change out of £30 million. Manet would have been amused; during his lifetime, he couldn't even get his pictures into exhibitions in France. He often painted bar scenes and was a noted bon viveur. As Bass was a famous export beer, it would have been a familiar sight to him.

Bass even made it to the American art scene. The noted portraitist Levi Wells Prentice painted *Still Life with Bass Ale*. Another Bass painting was recently sold in America for $17,000. It was by the Norfolk born British sporting artist, John Emms, and it shows a fox terrier with a plate with a bone on it and a quart bottle of Bass in the foreground. There are also well known paintings by Charles Spence Layh and Fred Elwell. One curiosity is a very fine painting entitled *Old Acquaintances* by JM Burfield, showing the village parson and a farmer being served with Bass by a girl. On the wall is an advertisement for J and C Burfield of the Phoenix Brewery, Hastings: Was Burfield a member of the family or was it just coincidence?

But the most famous devotee of Bass as a subject was Picasso. During the period from 1912 to 1915, when he was living in Paris, he produced no fewer than 14 paintings, constructions and collages featuring bottles of Bass. Most are now in the Picasso Museum in Paris and viewing them prompted a cynical friend of mine to remark that this was obviously the start of Picasso's Cubist period because he was so inspired by the contents of the bottles, he could only paint in squares when he had drunk the lot. Personally, I thought this was a bit much coming from a man who tried to drink straight from the bottle one night in a pub, only to find that it had a three masted schooner in it.

Picasso gave all his works nicely descriptive titles such as *Pipe, Bottle of Bass and Dice, Still Life with Bottle of Bass* and *Bottle of Bass, Glass and Newspaper*. Alas we shall not see his like again. It is difficult to imagine a modern artist titling his construction: *Can of lager, football yob and police officer* – doesn't have quite the same ring to it.

But let's finish with a real curiosity. Bass has even had a song written in its honour. I once picked up the sheet music for a music hall song called Bitter Beer. It contained the lines:

> I've tasted hock and claret too, Madeira and Moselle
> But not one of those boshy wines revives this languid swell
> Of all complaints from A to Z the fact is very clear
> There's no disease but what's been cured by Bass's Bitter Beer

Apparently it was 'sung nightly with immense success by Tom Maclagan'. I'll just bet it was.

Maurice Lovett died shortly after this article was finished so it has been left as written apart from style editing.

THE BRITISH INFLUENCE
Today St. Albans, tomorrow the world

BY MICHAEL JACKSON

It is like saying grace. In the wine cellars of Baron Bachofen von Echt, under his schloss at Nussdorf, on the edge of the Vienna woods, I have raised a glass of 'Sir Henry's' dry stout, brewed on the premises, and said a silent prayer of thanks to the Campaign for Real Ale. Under a windmill in Amsterdam, at the Egg Brewery, I have sampled an abbey-style ale called Ostrich and entertained the same thought. Over *une verre d'ambrée* at Les Brasseurs, in Lille, I have proffered my thanks before tucking into *coq à la biere* likewise before a glass of St Ambroise in Montreal.

An unfiltered, Vienna-style lager at Zip City, downstairs from the old offices of the National Temperance Society, in the Flat Iron district of Manhattan? Zip City's literary debt is to Sinclair Lewis, but there would have not been such brewpubs, lager or not, without the inspiration of the Campaign for Real Ale. An 'Irish' Ale at the Goose Island brewpub, in Chicago, or a 'Scottish' one in Sherlock's Home (in the suburbs of Minneapolis? Great Scot, Watson!) Come to that, an Irish Ale at Big Rock in Calgary or a Scottish one at Grant's in Yakima (the kind of town where they ask you to check your gun as well as your hat) in the Cascade Mountains. How can I or they ever repay our debts to CAMRA?

Is there no end to these delights? How about an Oyster Stout at the Pike Place Brewery, in Seattle; a Boysenberry Wheat Beer, at Rogue River, in Ashland, Oregon; a Big Foot Barley Wine, at Sierra Nevada, in Chico, California? Thank you, CAMRA. Thank you very much indeed.

I have sipped a fruity, Düsseldorf-style Altbier made by Sapporo, and

THE BRITISH INFLUENCE

served in the Lion Brasserie, under the Komatsu building in the Ginza district of Tokyo; a maltier interpretation of the same style at Suntory's experimental brewery in the horse-racing town of Fuchu City; and a rather caramelly version at Kirin's Spring Valley brewpub in Yokohama. Do the astonishingly skilled brewers of Japan know they owe a debt to CAMRA? Some do. You would be surprised.

In Melbourne, there was a wonderfully creamy milk stout, inappropriately called Razorback, at the Geebung Polo Club; near Canberra a much drier, thinner, stout made by Father Michael O'Halloran a catholic priest, at the Old Goulburn brewery at Picton, on the road to Sydney, the silky Burragorang Bock produced by a brewer called Deo Gratias Lule, born in Kenya but educated in malty magic in Edinburgh. Do I thank CAMRA once more? Yes, I do. Let me explain why.

When CAMRA was born, breweries were closing not only in Britain but also in the United States and most other parts of the developed world. The surviving breweries were making blander and blander beers, and fewer of them, not just in Britain, but almost everywhere else. Since prohibition in the United States, two world wars, and the growth of mass-marketing in the 1950s and 1960s, people had believed that a brewery was something that closed. They had convinced themselves that bland beer was inevitable.

The founders of CAMRA set out to save traditional breweries and beers, not to inspire new ones, but that was the effect of their efforts. They concerned themselves only with Britain, but their inspiration spread far and wide. Within three or four years of CAMRA's birth in 1971, new breweries were opening in Britain. Soon afterwards, they were starting all over the developed world.

The oldest type of brewery, that attached to a pub, had in Britain diminished in number to four, but scores have opened since then. Some have closed after a year or two, but there are today 50 or 60 in Britain. Inspired by that revival, Bert Grant (today a legend in American beer) opened his brewpub in the old opera house at Yakima, Washington. Down the coast, a kettle was fired in a 100-year-old saloon in the appropriately-named town of Hopland, in Mendocino county, California. Today there are 2,000 brewpubs and micros in the United States.

The other category of new small brewery is the tiny, free-standing, business. This is smaller than an old-established local or regional brewery, and more likely to produce speciality beers. Without the climate created by CAMRA, would Peter Austin have come out of retirement to establish the pioneering Ringwood brewery (famous for its Old Thumper)? I do not believe so for a moment. Austin went on to help establish micro-breweries elsewhere in Europe, all over North America, and even in China. Having girdled the New World, the movement came back to the Old, to Belgium and The Netherlands, and even to Germany, where a new generation of brewpubs joined the hundreds of long-established ones. At one of the earliest Great British Beer Festivals, I encountered a man named Jack McAuliffe, who had been in Britain with the United States Navy. He had been inspired by the Campaign for Real Ale, and was in the process of starting America's first micro-brewery, in Sonoma, California. He proved to be ahead of his time.

At another Great British Beer Festival I was approached by Gordon Bowker, one of the Berkeley generation of the 1960s. He had helped start an alternative newspaper, and a 'gourmet' coffee-roasting company, both in Seattle. He had sought me out to see whether I thought a micro-brewery would work in Seattle. I hope I encouraged him, though my memories are fogged by the beer we enjoyed together. The brewery he subsequently helped found, Red Hook, is today one of the most successful in America and Seattle the country's new beer capital.

We are talking here about inspiration not imitation. The man who runs the Red Door bar in Seattle may, like me, be a Lithuanian Yorkshireman, but his establishment sells fine (yes, cask-conditioned) beers that are definitely New American in their character.

Like the best of Britain's local, regional and national brewers, their counterparts in the United States (and other developed nations) have begun to offer a wider range of beers, including some genuine specialities. The country's oldest brewery, in Pottsville, Pennsylvania, once seemed set to close but today is prospering on the success of its celebrated porter. Even the country's biggest single brewery plant, Coors, in Golden, Colorado, makes a creditable Vienna-style lager, called Winterfest, as a seasonal special.

CAMRA's Great British Beer Festival has been an inspiration, too. In the early 1980s, a group of enthusiasts in Boulder, Colorado, started a similar Great American Beer Festival, open to brewpubs, micros, locals, regionals and national brewers. The festival soon moved to the bigger city of Denver, and has grown every year since.

CAMRA's monthly tabloid *What's Brewing* has inspired similar papers in Baltimore, New York, Minneapolis, Denver and San Francisco. There have even been efforts to launch glossy magazines for beer-lovers in Italy, France, Belgium, Britain itself, the United States, Canada and Australia.

CAMRA's annual *Good Beer Guide* has inspired more modest booklets in the US, and in Japan.

Without the celebration of beer by CAMRA, journalists, authors and television programme-makers would never have been emboldened to discuss in such detail their favourite products, nor editors accepted their essays. There is still less writing on beer than there is on wine, but you can nonetheless find the two alongside one another in some of the Saturday papers every other week. There is now such an animal as a beer-writer, not only in Britain but also in the United States, Belgium, and elsewhere.

On my own travels in search of beer I constantly meet brewers who have visited Britain to sample real ale, see how it's made, and make a pilgrimage to CAMRA's offices in the unlikely location of St Albans. When we greet one another, it is almost as though there should be some secret handshake. We feel as though we are in a resistance movement, fighting against Fear of Flavour. By the time the night is out, we will have commiserated over blandness in beer, bread, cheese – the fight is against a bland quality of life.

Many beer-lovers in the United States and elsewhere join CAMRA just so that they can stand up and be counted. There is little direct benefit for them. Attempts are being made to start something similar, but of more practical local application, in the US. There is a sister organisation in Canada, and there are counterparts in Scandinavia, The Netherlands and Belgium.

Then again, I meet new brewers and beer-lovers who have recently jumped on the dray and who have no idea where all this started. 'We've got all these great new breweries, they make fantastic beers!' enthuses a trucker in Tallahassee, a dentist in Dayton, a surfer in San Diego. 'Do you have anything like that in Europe?' I bite my tongue and smilingly nod assent. Four Britons started the whole thing, back in 1971.

Sure, the elements were universal, leisure was on the increase, and some found it in a new appreciation of food and drink; people were beginning to travel more, and discover the tastes of other nations; that new perspective also gave them a more appreciative view of their own heritage; conservation of architecture had spread to other aspects of life; consumers sought variety; the more discerning wanted authenticity, and demanded to know how a product was made, and what it contained; for some small was beautiful.

Many of us felt these impulses, but we thought nothing could be done, until the Famous Four proved us wrong. It was only then that we joined the battle.

Those friends who do not understand chide me: 'You used to write about more serious things; now it's all about beer.' Journalists imagine they can change the world. The founders of CAMRA did.

BRITISH BEER EXPORTS

BY MIKE RIPLEY

Diplomatic gifts of English ale were reputedly sent to the medieval Kings of France and were as much prized there as the finest French wines in England. Certainly by Tudor times London beer was following English troops on campaigns abroad and had become a staple item on board ships exploring and colonising the New World. Such beginnings flourished in the eighteenth century into a beer export trade which had effects on the British brewing industry far in excess of the actual volumes it represented. Because exports were never more than a small proportion of the rapidly-expanding domestic market their influence has often been overlooked.

Perhaps surprisingly it is America, first colonial then independent, which holds the record as the longest continuous customer for British beer (apart from the time of prohibition) although only the biggest since 1982. The trade with America came initially through the early colonists and then as an off-shoot of Britain's trade with the West Indies. Some of the earliest records of the London brewers show shipments to Barbados and America from 1695 and Samuel Whitbread is said to have sent his first consignment to New York in 1746, only four years after the establishment of his Chiswell Street Brewery. When the colonial break came in 1776 the first thing British troops in Boston did was to order 5,000 butts (108 gallon casks) of strong beer from London brewers Felix Calvert and Henry Thrale.

Most of the regular trade, which ran at about 9,000 barrels a year in 1775, would have been in strong dark beer and porter. George Washington was known to be particularly fond of porter but after 1776 he preferred a domestic brewed beer rather than taking succour from the enemy. Despite the imposition of import duties on British beer such as by Virginia (4d a gallon in 1786, raised to 9d in 1787)[1] and no doubt other states, trade with America actually doubled after the Revolution and continued to rise, albeit slowly, to about 24,000 barrels by 1870 and almost 70,000 by 1910.

There were problems along the way. That 'practical brewer' WL Tizard[2] recommended in the 1840s that the best beer for America was porter which had been 'vatted for the winter' before shipping, but warned of unscrupulous merchants diluting it with molasses and water! The Scottish brewer Younger had exported beer to America from 1836 and in 1856 sold a consignment of 60 hogsheads in auction immediately on landing in San Francisco.[3] But Younger's agents were worried about their good name and in the later 1850s took advertising space in St Louis newspapers to warn of the risk of confusion with 'Yonkers', a rival beer they clearly regarded as a poor imitation of their own.

There were happier tales: of Bass's ale being one of the brands available in the dining cars of transcontinental railroads and of Allsopp's ales winning medals at the Centennial Brewers Exhibition in Philadelphia in 1876. When the end of the trade came it was outside of brewer or consumer control although it is interesting to note that 28 barrels of British beer did get into the USA in 1919 before prohibition closed the door. After the repeal of prohibition in 1933, but more importantly since the 1970s, the renaissance of British beer exports to the US is a success story both in volume and imitation. Since 1982 the USA has been the biggest overseas customer of British beer and the volumes currently achieved there match the Indian trade of the last century at its peak. And within the USA the explosion of microbrewers has paid homage to British styles of brewing, adding to the interest in ale.

Although London porter and stout were probably sent to Russia in greater quantities the story of the Baltic trade is really the story of Burton-on-Trent. The reputation of well matured, strong, black London beers was established in Russia under the patronage of the Empress Catherine the Great. London porter and stout enjoyed such royal favour in the Tsarist court at St Petersburg that a particularly strong 'Imperial' or 'Russian' version of stout was developed for the market and is still brewed today in limited quantities.

But it was the nut-brown, sweet ale of Burton sent to Russia and Poland

and Prussia which was to prove more important. The trade with the Baltic countries, followed in the wake of porter and stout exports and became a 'trade' in the literal sense of the word. The early exponents of the Baltic trade, such as Benjamin Wilson (later Allsopp's) and William Worthington (now Bass), became not just salesmen but traders in Baltic goods. Ale exported to the Baltic, as long as it was ready by March, could be shipped relatively cheaply – almost as ballast – in return for much-in-demand imports such as iron, hemp, tallow and particularly wood. The timber imports alone created a flourishing sawyer and coopering industry around Burton as the wood, especially the oak, was cut and treated for, among other things, beer casks, as the 40-gallon casks used to send the ale were never returned.

By 1780 there were 13 brewers in Burton and some 40 per cent of production was for export, though in individual cases the importance of the Baltic trade was at times as high as 75 per cent of output.[4] Most were better known abroad than at home and some probably better known as Baltic traders and speculators, or even for their shipping interests, than as brewers. But from 1790 the French Revolution and Napoleonic wars disrupted and finally killed the trade. Having dealt with all the problems of quality control, shipping deadlines and even canal pirates, Burton brewers faced rising costs (especially wages as the labour force was attracted to factory-based industry or conscripted into the army or navy) and the political carving-up of their market. First Poland, then Russia, closed the doors on imported beer either by tariffs or for military reasons, which also increased insurance premiums.[5]

The port of Danzig remained a loyal customer throughout but the end came suddenly, after a brief peacetime revival, when Russia banned imports in 1822 and by 1826 had established breweries of her own. The Burton brewers were left with a type of beer – strong Burton ale – which, though highly regarded, was by no means as popular domestically as porter, debts they could not collect, and capital ensnared in useless casks and ships. Many went to the wall, but the ones who survived prospered. By 1830, less than ten years after the Baltic collapse, Bass was brewing 10,000 barrels a year of which more than 50 per cent was for export. The destination this time was India.

The Burton brewers saw the virtual monopoly on the Indian trade held by the London brewer Hodgson[6] and his light, sparkling 'India Ale'. There were clear possibilities of a growth market as British troops and administrators began to turn India into the centre of the developing British Empire.

There was also the distinct possibility that the brewers of Burton, with their highly favourable water supply (much harder water than London), could produce a lighter-coloured beer, better suited for drinking in tropical climes, than that from Hodgson's Bow Bridge site. Other London brewers had tried, such as Barclay in 1799.

Their chance came, fortuitously, in 1822 and 1823 when Hodgson refused to extend credit to his Indian merchants. No doubt a considerable amount of primitive industrial espionage took place to copy 'India Ale' and many breweries take the credit for developing the first India Pale Ale. ('Pale' because it was paler than ordinary ale). Whoever was the first, there were many who tried and by 1833, beer from Allsopp's, Bass, Barclay's, Tennent's in Glasgow and Charrington's in London, were vying with each other on the docks in Calcutta.

The trade rose from an estimated 20,000 barrels in 1840 to a peak of 217,000 barrels in 1870 and by 1860, pale ale was rated the 'first consideration' in the Allsopp's brewery. So successful was this new beer that Hodgson's trade had virtually disappeared by 1840. The Burton brewers quickly refined the techniques of using lighter malts, heavier hopping rates and more careful fermentation needed to get the beer to India in good condition – a crucial factor as the agitation of a sea voyage and the heat of the tropics could easily have spelled disaster. A Calcutta merchant wrote to WL Tizard that 'the ale adapted for this market should be clear, light, bitter, pale ale of a moderate strength'. In the brewing press recipes and formulae abounded. William Black[7] recommended an original gravity of 1060° – about half that for ale at the time! Others recommended hopping rates some ten times those used today, although the alpha content of the hops and their utilisation would be much less efficient than now.

Other brewers adopted the IPA techniques for export to other markets. Simond's of Reading, for example, began in 1834 to brew 'a novel kind of beer, pale ale, for export'[8] which reputedly travelled well on the six month journey to Australia. Simond's were to use this experience, and their military contacts, after nearby Aldershot became the home of the British army in 1872, to supply beer to troops abroad, not just in India, but in Malta in 1875 and Gibraltar in 1881 and later Egypt, Cyprus and South Africa.

Yet the importance of India Pale Ale lay in the domestic British market. India as a market began to decline after 1870 as trade with Australia and New Zealand flourished. It was the beer, not the export of it, which provided a turning point in the fortunes of the British industry. The legend of how IPA was first tried at home are legion. The most common is that a shipwreck off Liverpool in 1827 landed a batch of IPA destined for Calcutta by accident and it was quickly and gratefully consumed by the local inhabitants. Whatever the truth, IPA's fame spread and was undoubtedly boosted in popularity by the abolition of excise duty on glass in 1845 which provided the drinker with a vessel through which he could actually see his beer. The clear, sparkling qualities of the pale ales of Burton obviously held more visual appeal than the dark, thick porters and the hoppy bitterness appealed over the rather sweeter taste of a conventional ale. In 1854 the Newcastle bottler Alex Laing was offering 'Pale India Beer' at 2s.6d per dozen quarts and also 'High-Hopped India Pale Ale' at 4s. per dozen – fantastic price premiums compared to the locally-brewed mild ales.[9]

By the 1850s the brewers had further developed 'running bitter' versions for sale on draught to the expanding urban population and the expression 'pint of bitter' entered the English language – and also sounded the death-knell of porter as the staple drink. It is also arguable that this change in drinking habits – from dark beers to paler ales – cushioned Britain from the revolution in lager-style beers which was taking place in central Europe and was eventually to sweep the world leaving only Britain and Ireland producing a majority of their beer in the top fermented traditions of ales and stouts. From this period on, however, British beer became, internationally, a minority taste. Lager beers rapidly spread throughout Europe and America and were to conquer the markets of South America, Australasia and, ironically, India.

British beer exports peaked in the years immediately before the Great War with the figures for 1911, 1912 and 1913 all in excess of 600,000 barrels, considerably above the average pattern recorded in the previous fifty years. These three years, however, are unrepresentative and the increases in them must be down to increasing troop, and particularly naval, build-ups in view of rising international tension. One observer[10] noted in 1905 that 'the amount of beer exported has not advanced to any extent during the last thirty years'.

Wartime demands on shipping and U-boat action and government interference in the amount of beer brewers could produce, all combined to reduce the export trade and to change it. Virtually all markets, except military ones, closed during the war or, at least, were severely curtailed. If military conditions are ignored, the real situation was that in the last years of truly peaceful trading, around 1910, exports were in the order of 590,000 barrels. After the war, in 1920, the levels steadied at around 300,000.

Exports had dropped by almost 50 per cent because of the war and the markets had changed.

India, which took 100,000 barrels in 1912, was down to 14,000 by 1918 and the trade was never to recover its former volumes. Australia and New Zealand, more significantly, fell from a 1912 volume of 123,000 barrels to 6,000 in the same period and, in the absence of British beer, native industries emerged. Closer to home, the founding of the Irish Republic meant that it became an export market although it also began to export stout in its own right from 1922. Throughout the 1920s the average exports were little more than 300,000 barrels a year and, in the depression years of the early 1930s, this had fallen to 220,000. There was some recovery in 1938, when levels rose to 329,400 barrels, but whilst the second world war boosted British domestic production it played havoc with exports other than those for troops stationed abroad.

The main post-war market in the late 1940s turned out to be Belgium, a country still very loyal to the ale tradition of brewing and one which was to remain Britain's biggest customer for 30 years. In the period 1949 to 1955 exports averaged 252,000 barrels a year. After Belgium the developing, and soon to be independent, British territories in West Africa were the best customers. India, partitioned and independent in 1947, said goodbye not only to the Raj, but to British beer, the trade falling to below 5,000 barrels. American servicemen also appeared to have no taste for British beer for, despite the millions who used Britain's pubs during the war, few demanded the beer 'back home'. The twin legacy of prohibition in the USA and post-war rationing and shortages in the UK did nothing to promote British beer there above a 1,400 barrels a year average.

From 1956 to 1974 exports averaged a steady 440,000 barrels a year, despite total domestic production increasing from 24 million barrels to 38 million in the same period. Belgium remained the biggest customer although Malaysia and Singapore came close in the early 1960s taking some 92,000 barrels. But once British troops were removed from Malaya beer exports fell accordingly. And then Belgium, like the rest of continental Europe, swung over to a majority lager drinking market and by the mid-1970s UK exports had dropped to a level no higher than that of the 1850s.[11]

The revival began in 1978 and came from two sources. Firstly, British brewers, through the Brewers' Society, targeted specific export markets and the first target selected was the United States. Previously brewers had exported along colonial routes or to where there were, or had been, British forces overseas – some 200 plus destinations. By joining together in a generic 'Beer from Britain' campaign, using the image of the pub and supplying draught beer, in fewer markets, a much greater impact was achieved, certainly in the United States, following trade exhibitions in Atlanta, San Francisco, New Orleans, and other major cities. Exports to the US increased tenfold between 1975 and 1995 from around 50,000 barrels a year to almost half a million, and the current target market for British brewers is Japan.

The second prong of the export revival came, unexpectedly, from Italy. In 1978 Italian beer buffs began to collect the commemorative ales brewed to mark the Silver Jubilee of the Queen's Coronation, and collect them in a big way. And not only collect them, but drink them! Most Jubilee beers were strong ales or barley wines, types of beer unknown in Italy but very rapidly and affectionately appreciated. On the back of this consumer interest (further boosted by Royal Wedding Ales in 1981) a flourishing export trade grew up. Apart from Ireland, Italy is now the most important market for British beer within the European Union.

Throughout the 1980s exports grew significantly, passing the one million barrel milestone in 1991, something never achieved even at the height of the British Empire. It is quite conceivable that the 2,000,000 barrel mark will be reached quite soon. For a country which brews types of beer which no other does, and which has a draught beer culture which few others do, and which is an island, making transport of bulky, perishable items very expensive, that would be no mean achievement.

References

(1) *Brewed in America*, Stanley Baron (Boston, 1962)
(2) *The Theory and Practice of Brewing*, WL Tizard (London 1846)
(3) *The Younger Centuries*, David Keir (1951)
(4) *Burton Upon Trent*, CC Owen (1978)
(5) *Pale Ale and Bitter Beer*, Staffordshire County Council (1977)
(6) *The Brewing Industry in England, 1700 – 1832*, Peter Mathias (1960)
(7) *A Practical Treatise on Brewing*, William Black (1849)
(8) *The Road to Worton Grange*, TAB Corley (1981)
(9) *Brewers and Bottlers of Newcastle*, Brian Bennison (1995)
(10) *The Brewing Industry*, Julian L Baker (London, 1905)
(11) *British Beer Abroad*, MD Ripley (*The Brewer*, August 1986)

TRANSATLANTIC TASTE
One Yank's view of British beer

BY BENJAMIN MYERS

At a recent Conference of Brewers, Lord Burton claimed that his country won its high and proud position among the nations of the Earth simply on the account of its characteristic dietary, 'beef and beer'. Whereupon someone made the waggish comment, 'Why drag in the beef?' A.F.W. Hackwood, 1910.

Unlike many devotees of fine British beer, I cannot remember either the name or the exact taste of my first pint. I can, however, remember the circumstances; the first evening I ever sampled cask-conditioned ale. It was the beginning of January, 1991. I'd just arrived, with about 30 of my American college peers, for a two-term university exchange program at Oxford. After allowing us to drop off our luggage, an older Oxford student (who was our in-house guide to the city and university) roused us all for an evening of 'pubbing.' The scene must have been every British beer-lover's nightmare: 30 jet-lagged American students, some of us (including me) not old enough to drink legally in our home country, on a guided tour of Oxford city-centre pubs. First up was The Turf, a tiny half-timbered tavern reputedly visited by Shakespeare and certainly recorded as the setting of a pivotal scene in Hardy's *Jude the Obscure*.

I can't remember The Turf's draught selection, nor do I remember being much surprised by the hand-pumps used to pour the beers (I'd seen enough British TV shows back home). But I recall sitting with my fellow students in the pub's garden, warming ourselves next to the large coal-burning pots put outside during wintry weather, enjoying a beer unlike any I'd tasted before. It had colour! It had character! Flavour! Aftertaste! Aroma! And no bloating carbonation. It slipped down as quickly and as quietly as I did later that evening, having sampled more of the same at The Kings Arms and a few other local watering holes.

Over the next several weeks, a group of us made it our primary evening business to continue these bibulous explorations. Moreover, later that spring, my roommate and I spent a significant portion of a trip around Scotland guided by the pages of Camra's *Good Beer Guide* (which we thought was simply amazing – an entire book about good beer!) And it is no exaggeration to say that my taste for real British beer prompted me to search out the same qualities in American suds, to discover my country's now famous 'microbrewing revolution', and to return to Britain for a year of further beer-related 'studies'.

Since then, my tastebuds have tackled a broad range of beer-styles from across the world: one-year-old lambic straight from its wooden barrel, authentic Bavarian Weissbier as brewed in Colorado, Sri Lankan stout, Belgian 'Scotch' ales, and many, many others. But I keep returning to Britain whenever an opportunity arises. There's something about (properly treated) cask-conditioned ale that places it in a category by itself. Now don't get me wrong: I'm not a cask ale *uber alles* kind of guy. It's just that, at least until recently, the most distinctive British beers always were available on draught in cask-conditioned form. There are several notable exceptions – Worthington White Shield, Courage Imperial Russian Stout, Gale's Prize Old Ale, Lee's Moonraker, and Fowler's Wee Heavy, to name a few – but, overall, cask ales have been the standard-bearers of modern British brewing.

I once tried to articulate the key to cask ale's character during a pause between pints of Theakston's fruity Masham Ale at an annual Camra meeting: 'the glory of cask-conditioning as a process,' I ventured, 'is that it imparts a roundness and depth to beer that otherwise is extremely difficult to achieve.' That's not to say, of course, that cask conditioning automatically makes British ales the cream of the beery crop. As a category, artisanal Belgian brews tend to far outstrip their cross-Channel counterparts – and most of the world's other beers – in terms of character and distinctive flavour. Several American microbrewers also supply suds that put British ales to shame. And there are plenty of world-class lagers which simply have no English, Scottish or Welsh equal.

So why do I keep returning to British beer? The answer, in part, lies with the 'honesty' of cask ale. If it's produced by an established regional brewery, it probably has been made in almost the same way for the better part of a century – and often times much longer. At Sam Smith's Brewery in Tadcaster (and at many other regionals) you'll even find local families who have been working for the company through several generations! With that much tradition and experience behind each pint, drinkers can feel pretty confident that their beer is gimmick-free. There are no surprises, no disappointments, just good 'old-fashioned' ale. The breweries know exactly what they are making, and their customers know what to expect. Granted, Anheuser-Busch also knows what it's making. And Budweiser drinkers know what they're getting. But the basic products from America's major brewers, and from most 'mega-brewers' across the world, always have had far less character than the average pint of cask ale. Nobody waxes lyrical over 'good old-fashioned American-style Pilsner'. Or, for that matter, bland British kegged and canned beer. On the other hand, there is some truth to the argument that the traditional nature of British brewing has forestalled beery innovation. It's hard to imagine Timothy Taylor's launching a raspberry-flavoured, unfiltered wheat beer, for example, or Robinson's introducing a long-lagered doppelbock. Thankfully, the past several years have seen not only the birth of many creative 'microbrewers' throughout Britain, but also the (re)introduction of seasonal and special beers by older breweries. These products probably are as refreshing for brewers to make as they are for consumers to drink. The same goes for Britain's new wave of bottled (and bottle-conditioned) beers.

    These novel brews aside, British ales deserve praise for their consistently-high level of flavour relative to the workaday suds of other countries. A standard draught ale from a standard British brewer, as suggested above, fits the description 'flavourful beer'. While only a few regularly rise to the heights of distinctive character – it's no surprise that certain brands repeatedly take top honours at beer festivals – the great body of British ale, overall, is quite tasty. I know that if I walk into any pub where the cellarman is up to his (or her) job, I'm going to receive an enjoyable, rewarding pint. This situation is almost unique to Britain.

    Sometimes pub-goers can get particularly lucky. A friend and I left our London office one night, I remember, with plans to 'pop in for a swift pint' at a Young's house up the road. Upon arrival, we discovered that the landlord had just tapped a fresh cask of Young's 'ordinary' Bitter. There was nothing ordinary about it! The ale was so fresh, so tangy, so full of life and flavour that we spent the better part of the evening (including dinner at the pub) toasting its virtues. Just thinking about it makes me thirsty. That evening's wonderful character is attributable, in a great part, to Young's beer. But the convivial atmosphere of the pub also played an important role. In fact, my ongoing love for British beer is grounded in an appreciation of good pubs: I never enjoy traditional ale as much as when I'm sharing a round with friends at a favoured 'local'. Even the Great British Beer Festival, with its stunning selection of more than 300 cask-conditioned brews, can't replicate this feeling.

I am aware that a lot of pubs are hated for their 'pretentious atmosphere' or 'fake decor', and I know that Britain also has its share of dismal 'backstreet boozers.' But I'd take a British pub any day over one of the windowless corner bars so frequently found in American cities. Or even over a Czech tavern or a Bavarian biergarten. Nowhere else have I found such a socially-oriented atmosphere for enjoying flavourful beer. A good pub and a good pint can make the most difficult day brighter, the best day even better.

It is extremely disappointing that pubs are suffering as people increasingly choose to drink at home. On the positive side, however, this changing market appears to have prompted British brewers to introduce more distinctive products both for take-home and for their remaining outlets. Think of it this way: although 'widgeted cans' do not deliver the full flavour of draught beer, there's no question that they offer better presentation than standard fizzy canisters. And the rise of premium draught brews (developed to capitalise on new 'moderate' drinking habits) surely has enlivened many a hand-pump. The overall situation actually may work out in the consumer's favour. Therefore, even though fine British beer faces many challenges (not the least of which is the country's exorbitant duty), I feel confident that I'll always be able to find a delicious pint during future visits. The reason is simple: all across the world, people are rediscovering a taste for distinctive beer. From America to Australia, from Toronto to Tokyo, characterful brews are hot news.

This certainly is the case in Britain. British breweries are rising to the challenge. And nothing – not keg beer, not 'nitrokeg' ales, not cross-Channel bootlegging – is going to stem the flavoursome, frothy tide.

UK BEER EXCISE DUTY
A brief history

BY PETER OGIE

Throughout history governments of every persuasion have always been convinced that they can spend taxpayers' money better than the taxpayers themselves. They have taken every opportunity to raise taxes by direct or indirect means in order to finance the newest policy or the latest emergency. The imposition of a tax on the production or use of a material or article has been standard practice for hundreds of years. Beer has not been immune from such an imposition, a tax on 'brewers moveables' being recorded in the twelfth century. However, it was not until 1643 when, as a temporary measure, and in order to pay for the Civil War, that such a tax became formally established and inevitably permanent. The Board of Excise was not formed until 1683, so brewing has the unenviable distinction of being the oldest of the excise trades. However, at that time malt and hops were also taxed so the ultimate consumer had to suffer in three ways. Thank goodness value added tax was not around at that time as well!

Even in these early days duty was charged on the strength of the beer, there being two strengths recognised, 'strong' and 'small' and these were distinguished by their selling price. This made them clearly susceptible to fraud since small beer carried only a quarter of the duty of the strong and enabled the less-than-honest brewer to mix the two and to sell the mixture as strong. To go some way to prevent this the government fixed a maximum price for small beer and gave excise officers the necessary powers to test the product. 'The gauger may taste the product upon any brewer's dray.' In practical terms the brewer was requested to attend at his local excise office at prescribed times where he declared the quantities and types of beer for which he was liable, paid the respective duty and received a warrant authorising disposal of the beer. In 1660 excise officers began visiting breweries to establish better control, a procedure that remained in place until 1985. This duty was inequitable since it was imposed only on beer made for sale. Brewers who brewed solely for themselves were exempt. It is apparent that these methods of imposing and collecting this duty were unsound and open to abuse, and led to friction between brewers and excise officers, so in 1830 beer duty was abolished. But the duties on malt and hops remained.

The situation continued unaltered until 1862 when the hop duty was repealed and in 1880 the then Chancellor of the Exchequer, Mr Gladstone, repealed the malt tax and replaced it with a new duty on beer which was intended to raise the same revenue as the malt duty. He now had the technology to help him. In 1777 John Richardson published *Treatise on the Saccharometer* which was to revolutionise brewing practice and permit brewers to exercise a much greater control over their processes and to improve their record keeping. In 1847 Dobson and Phillips established a method for determining the original gravity of beer. Gladstone was therefore able to base his new duty on a measurable parameter, the specific gravity of wort. At that time, and on average, a quarter of malt would yield 4 barrels of beer at 1055° which was to be known as standard gravity. A duty rate at this standard gravity was fixed, and the charge was made on the equivalent volume at the standard gravity calculated from a brewery's total production at many different gravities. There were two conditions applied: one to safeguard the brewers, whereby it was understood that losses of material occur during the brewing process, so that duty would be charged on only 94 per cent of the volume of wort declared. Thus the 6 per cent wastage allowance came into being. The other, to safeguard the Revenue, was the materials charge, to give the excise officers the right to levy duty on the quantity of beer deemed to have been produced from the materials used, if for any reason, it exceeded the brewer's declaration. However, in discussions with the Industry which preceded the introduction of this duty, the brewers convinced Mr Gladstone that standard gravity should be 1057°, and this he reluctantly accepted, only for a subsequent chancellor to change it back to 1055° in 1889.

This system of duty then remained relatively unchanged for another 100 years or so. There was one minor amendment when in 1915 a change in the law provided relief from duty on beer which had accidentally become spoilt or otherwise unfit for use after it had left brewery entered premises, and on its return to those entered premises. This was known as the returned spoilt beer relief. For the duty on this to be calculated it was necessary to be able to determine the specific gravity of the wort from which the beer had been made. A method for measuring this OG, as it was called, was published at about this time by Thorpe and Brown, the former representing His Majesty's Customs and Excise and the latter representing the industry. This impressive piece of practical work resulted in an empirical table giving the relationship between analytical figures for the specific gravity of beer, the specific gravity of the alcoholic distillate from the beer and the OG of the wort from which the beer was produced. As this was based on experimental results, and was inevitably an average, 3 to 4° was deducted from the result to exclude any possible outliers. This method remains today the reference method to be used in the event of any dispute between HMCE and traders, although whether many have the skill to perform it is open to doubt.

There was another anomaly in the system: it was not linear. There was a minimum gravity on which duty was charged. Any worts declared at gravities lower than this minimum would attract this minimum charge. This minimum gravity varied over the years between 1027°–1030° until it was abolished in 1974 and duty became linear.

Although the duty system remained unchanged the duty rate did not. On introduction the rate was 6/3d (31p) per barrel at standard gravity. By 1900 it had increased to 7/9d (40p) at which it remained until 1920 when it was subject to a huge increase to 70/- (£3.50) and it stayed at around this figure until 1940 when it was increased from 80/- (£4.00) to £7.00 overnight. From then on the inexorable rise continued with a reduction in 1974 on the introduction of and to compensate for VAT, until in 1990 it has reached £87.312 per barrel at standard gravity. All this, compared with other taxes, has been very cheap for the Government to collect at approximately 3 per cent of the tax collected, but as income to the Exchequer it has been vital. For example in 1993 the beer duty together with beer VAT totalled £4,303m.

The next major change occurred in 1985. This was not a change of system but a change of control. Up to this date it had been the responsibility of the excise officer to control the system. He was required to check the brewer's declarations in the official excise book, his gravities and his dips and to gauge any vessels. He had the legal right to inspect any document and had access to all areas and to all records. It was his responsibility to calculate, on a monthly basis, the duty payable and to receive that amount on the 25th of the following month. In 1985 all that changed and the era of self assessment dawned. It became the brewer's responsibility to keep adequate records, not necessarily in the official excise book, maybe on a computer, to cause the vessels to be gauged and to calculate the duty payable himself. This was all subject to the necessary checks and balances introduced by HMCE but it certainly lightened the latter's load and gave the brewers greater flexibility to adopt changes in materials or processes.

This flexibility in process was not the only issue that had been exercising the brewer's minds. During the 1980s the larger brewers and the more efficient brewers all introduced duty management programmes, their object being to reduce the duty payable to a minimum whilst remaining within the law. They were able to take advantage of two concepts which had become anomalous, the 6 per cent wastage allowance and the Thorpe and Brown tables. With the former brewers became expert in reducing their actual wastage drastically, it is alleged in some cases to nil. By good housekeeping, by preventing losses through spillages, drips and accidents and by judicious investment in re-cycling plant some were able to reduce their wastage significantly. Indeed technology improved to such an extent that some were able to recover by distillation an aqueous alcohol solution from their surplus yeast, which they added back to their beer.

The Thorpe and Brown tables presented a genuine opportunity. Since they were devised experimentally early in the century and based on the production of ales by top fermentation in shallow vessels they could not strictly apply to the production of lagers by bottom fermentation in deep vessels. Accordingly, such terms as 'lager gain', 'hydrolysis gain' and 'dilution gain' entered the brewer's vocabulary and techniques such as pre-pitching, reduction of wort solids and use of high maltose syrups were shown to be beneficial from a duty perspective.

It was hardly surprising, therefore, that when the opportunity arose, through the European Union harmonisation legislation, HMCE were anxious to adopt an end product duty system which would remove all of these anomalies at a stroke. Thus in 1993 an entirely new system was introduced. In this case the duty is levied on the percentage of alcohol by volume (% abv) in the beer as it leaves the brewer's entered premises. In practical terms it is controlled by self-assessment on sophisticated computer systems with inbuilt cross-checks, and is subject to audit by excise officers. It includes special arrangements for dealing with cask-conditioned ales to take account of the possible increase in alcohol content after leaving entered premises and for the amount of sediment in the cask.

At present this first stage in the harmonisation process appears to have worked to everybody's satisfaction. Let us hope that, as consumers, the next stage, the overall reduction in UK beer duty, is not too long delayed.

BEER IN LITERATURE

BY JOHN BRICE

Beer has always been a good inspiration to writers. People like William Shakespeare, Charles Dickens, George Orwell, AA Milne, Dylan Thomas, Samuel Pepys, William Thackeray, PG Wodehouse, Jack London and many more all introduced drinking into their literary work in one form or another.

AA Milne was clear in his mind about the importance of the pub when he penned these few words in *An Ordnance Map*:

> Two inches to the north-west is written a word full of meaning – the most purposeful word that can be written on a map. 'Inn'.

He was truly speaking from the heart, or, at least, somewhere near the bottom of the glass. It's not clear how much effect drink had on the Christopher Robin and Winnie the Pooh stories he wrote because it never gets a mention in his works.

Charles Dickens, on the other hand, hardly wrote a chapter without the word 'Inn' appearing in it somewhere along the line. *The Pickwick Papers* was dedicated to the subject. His thoughts on the changing character of pubs in London pre-echoes some of the concerns still voiced today. He wrote this about the White Hart:

> There are in London several old inns, once the headquarters of celebrated coaches in the days when coaches performed their journeys in a graver and more solemn manner than they do in these times; but

which have now degenerated into little more than the abiding and booking places of country wagons. The reader would look in vain for any of these ancient hostelries, among the Golden Crosses and Bull and Mouths, which rear their stately fronts in the improved streets of London. If he would light upon any of these old places, he must direct his steps to the obscurer quarters of town; and there in some secluded nooks he will find several, still standing with a kind of gloomy sturdiness, amidst the modern innovations which surround them. In the Borough especially, there still remain some half dozen old inns, which have preserved their external features unchanged, and which have escaped alike the rage for public improvement, and the encroachments of private speculation. Great, rambling, queer, old places they are, with galleries, and passages, and staircases, wide enough and antiquated enough to furnish materials for a hundred ghost stories ....

And Dickens must have been painting a picture of his perfect pub when he wrote these words:

> How beautiful the landscape kindling in the light, and that luxuriant influence passing on like a celestial presence, brightening everything ...Cornfields, hedge-rows, fences, homesteads, and clustered roofs, the steeple of the church, the stream, the water-mill, all sprang out of the gloomy darkness smiling. At such a time, one little roadside inn, snugly sheltered behind a great elm-tree with a rare seat for idlers encircling its capacious bole, addressed a cheerful front towards the traveller, as a house of entertainment ought, and tempted him with many mute but significant assurances of a comfortable welcome. The ruddy sign-board perched up in the tree, with its golden letters winking in the sun, ogled the passer-by, from among the green leaves, like a jolly face, and promised good cheer. The horse-trough, full of clear, fresh water, and the ground below it sprinkled with droppings of fragrant hay, made every horse that passed prick up its ears. The crimson curtains in the lower rooms, and the pure white hangings in the little bed-chambers above, beckoned 'Come in!' with every breath of air. Upon the bright green shutters there were golden legends about beer and ale, and neat wines, and good beds; and an affecting picture of a brown jug frothing over at the top. Upon the window-sills were flowering plants in bright red pots, which made a lively show against the white front of the house; and

in the darkness of the doorway there were streaks of light which glanced off from the surface of bottles and tankards.

It is clear from those two descriptions of drinking houses what Dickens liked and disliked about where he chose to spend his time.

One wonders what drinking experiences William Shakespeare had lived through before writing the porter scene from Macbeth:

> Enter Macduff and Lennox.
> *Macduff* Was it so late, friend, ere you went to bed, that you do lie so late?
> *Porter* Faith, sir, we were carousing till the second cock; and drink, sir, is a great provoker of three things.
> *Macduff* What three things does drink especially provoke?
> *Porter* Marry, sir, nose painting, sleep and urine. Lechery, sir, it provokes and it unprovokes; it provokes the desire, but it takes away the performance; therefore, much drink may be said to be an equivocator with lechery; it makes him, and it mars him; it sets him on, and it takes him off; it persuades him, and disheartens him, makes him stand to, and not stand to; in conclusion, equivocates him in a sleep, and giving him the lie, leaves him.
> *Macduff* I believe drink gave thee the lie last night.
> *Porter* That it did, sir, i'the very throat o'me; but I required him for his lie; and, I think, being too strong for him, though he took up my legs sometime, yet I made a shift to cast him.

Samuel Pepys knew what was good for him when it came to having a drink. In the his diary he made this entry for 5 March 1668:

> To Westminster, where I found myself come time enough, and my brethren all ready. But I full of thoughts and trouble touching the issue of this day; and to comfort myself did go to the Dog and drink half-a-pint of mulled sack, and in the hall did drink a dram of brandy at Mrs Hewlett's; and with the warmth of this did find myself in better order as to courage, truly.

Maybe when journalist and writer Jerome K Jerome put pen to paper in *Three Men in a Boat* he had sampled the odd pint before. However, it appears the drinking efforts of his character, Harris, were not being appreciated when he wrote this:

> She was nuts on public houses, was England's Virgin Queen. There's

scarcely a pub of any attraction within ten miles of London that she does not seem to have looked in at, or stopped at, or slept at some time or other. I wonder now, supposing Harris, say, turned over a new leaf and became a great and good man, and got to be Prime Minister, and died, if they would put up signs over the public-houses that he had patronised: 'Harris had a glass of beer in this house'; 'Harris had two of Scotch cold here in the summer of '88'; 'Harris was chucked from here in December 1886'.

No there would be too many of them! It would be the houses that he had never entered that would become famous. 'Only house in South London that Harris never had a drink in!' The people would flock to it to see what could have been the matter with it

In 1695 the Prince Regent was clearly another with a keen nose for a good pint and someone who thought everyone should share his enthusiasm. At the time he said:

Beer and beef has made us what we are.

That was well before mad cow disease could have clouded his judgement.

Hilaire Belloc was the author of nonsense verse for children around the turn of the last century, but he also partook in adult pastimes if this quote of his is to be believed:

When you have lost your inns, drown your empty selves, for you will have lost the last of England.

George Borrow travelled through Europe and the East on foot writing about his experiences and knowledge of languages. As an Englishman, he certainly put that latter skill to good use with these words:

Good ale is the true and proper drink of the Englishman.

It is not just locals who enjoy British pubs and their beer. In 1129 an ambassador from Germany on a trip to England wrote:

The inns of England are the best in Europe, those in Canterbury are the best in England, and the Fountain, wherein I am now lodged as handsomely as I was in the King's Palace, the best in Canterbury.

The poet, John Keats, used his skill to look back to the great days of Elizabethan England when a group of men met at the Mermaid Tavern in

London, near the theatre of the same name. William Shakespeare, Ben Jonson, Christopher Marlowe and Francis Beaumont all used it at one time, which prompted Keats to write:

> Souls of poets dead and gone,
> What Elysium have ye known,
> Happy field or mossy cavern,
> Choicer than the Mermaid Tavern?

Although William Makepeace Thackeray was better known as a novelist and essayist, he did write this poem *To Peggy – a Barmaid* – obviously about one who took his fancy:

> See her as she moves,
> Scarce the ground she touches,
> Airy as a fay,
> Graceful as a duchess.
> Bare her rounded arm is,
> Bare her little leg is,
> Vestris never showed
> Ankles like to Peggy's.
> Braided is her hair,
> Soft her look and modest.
> Slim her little waist,
> Comfortably bodiced.

A regular frequenter of pubs and inns was Doctor Samuel Johnson. His writings have many references to ale houses, but this probably sums up his thoughts perfectly:

> There is nothing which has yet been contrived by man, by which so much happiness is produced as by a good tavern or inn.

George Orwell wrote about his favourite yet fictional public house, The Moon under Water, in the *London Evening Standard* on 9th February 1946. One of his treats was to have lunch there. He went on:

> The special pleasure of the lunch is that you can have draught stout with it. I doubt whether as many as ten per cent of London pubs serve draught stout, but The Moon under Water is one of them. It is a soft, creamy sort of stout, and it goes better in a pewter pot.
>
> They are particular about their drinking vessels at The Moon under

Water and never, for example, make the mistake of serving a pint in a handleless glass. Apart from glass and pewter mugs, they have some of those pleasant strawberry-pink china ones which are now seldom seen in London. China mugs went out about thirty years ago, because most people like their drink to be transparent, but in my opinion beer tastes better out of china.

Jack London's book, *John Barleycorn*, was described as one of the first intelligent literary studies of heavy drinking. Jack London was certainly a heavy drinker. His critics called him a self-confessed drunk, but he never liked being called an alcoholic. In the last chapter of *John Barleycorn* he wrote about a spell at sea when he did not touch a drop. He went on:

> On this long, five-month's voyage, I found that among all my bodily needs not the slightest shred of a bodily need for alcohol existed. But this I did find: my need was mental and social. When I thought of fellowship, the connotation was alcohol. Fellowship and alcohol were Siamese twins. They always occurred linked together.

He then went on to list the wonderful places he had visited around the world, the friends he had met and the drinks he had enjoyed. He concluded:

> And so I pondered my problem. I should not care to revisit all these fair places of the world except in the fashion I visited them before. Glass in hand! There is a magic in the phrase. It means more than all the words in the dictionary can be made to mean.

When it comes to writing, an epitaph can be the source of clever and amusing stuff. It could so easily apply to Jack London and so many others aforemetioned:

> Poor John Scott lies buried here;
> Tho' once he was both hale and stout,
> Death stretched him on his bitter bier,
> In another world he hops about.

One-liners are popular because they are so easy to remember. PG Wodehouse used this line in *The Inimitable Jeeves*:

> It was my uncle George who discovered that alcohol was a food well in advance of modern medical thought.

But the last thought rests with Dylan Thomas from *Under Milk Wood*.

Now here was a man who admitted being ejected from many pubs, and not always at closing time. So it was probably appropriate that he wrote these words:

> Up the street, in the Sailors Arms, Sinbad Sailors, grandson of Mary Ann Sailors, draws a pint in the sunlit bar. The ship's clock in the bar says half-past eleven. Half-past eleven is opening time. The hands of the clock have stayed still at half-past eleven for fifty years. It is always opening time in the Sailors Arms.

THE BRITISH PUBLIC HOUSE

BY PETER HAYDON

Once, enough years ago now for me to be old enough to use such an opening sentence, I went on summer holiday with my French copain to his family's time-share villa in Perpignan. One excursion took us to visit friends in a nearby village. It was fiesta time, in the centre of the dusty village square was a fountain. Old men in oversized Catalan berets would sit around its perimeter and, leaning forward, turn a clear glass of Ricard or Pastis cloudy with water. I, age twelve, had my own glass of Pastis and water, a treat indeed for a young English boy to whom alcohol was taboo. An accordion was produced and the people of the village formed a large circle around the fountain. They danced, young and old together. It was a Catalan dance and everyone knew it. I had seen nothing like it.

A dozen or so years later I went on holiday to Spain I took my guitar with me. The Spanish girls loved it. The sight of a young Englishman who wanted to play Sevillianas – albeit excruciatingly – was, to them, enchanting (so different from the Union Jack, boxered specimens of our race they were used to). They danced for me as I played, dances they had learnt in the streets of Cordoba when they had barely learnt to walk.

These images have always stayed with me for they remind me that we have no popular, participatory culture in Britain, no national costume, no folk tunes that identify us, no dances that betray our region of origin, nothing that is not kept alive by enthusiasts as a minority interest. Yet we do have the pub.

Activities in modern Britain are increasingly defined in terms of age. Today more than ever before the generations are isolated from each other. Funerals of princesses apart, it is only in the pub, or on the terraces (and possibly the pantomime) that it is still possible to enjoy shared experiences which cut across all age groups. For this reason, if for no other, the pub is a unique institution, which performs a number of functions that are crucial to the well-being of our society, and which we ignore at our great peril.

To foreigners Britain is defined by two institutions the monarchy and the pub. Both have often been under attack sometimes by the same people. The same people who cut off a King's head in 1649 also closed thousands of alehouses. Both institutions are currently having a hard time, but on this occasion both are being attacked from within. The general vulgarisation of British culture that is having such destructive effects in royal circles, is also enabling a bastardisation of the British pub to occur at an ever accelerating pace. A general sclerotic fatalism ensures that the process goes unchallenged. The indifference of the British to the state of their surroundings, is most alarming. We have adopted a tabloid mentality that allows us to wrap ourselves in the flag and sneer at the foreigner, but refuses to accept that the flag looks increasingly threadbare.

The pub is the mirror of our culture. If we are a yobbish society then our pubs are full of yobbish behaviour, if we are a caring society then the pub is the natural habitat of people who care. The pub is the crucible of British society, and its ubiquity and mundanity disguise the significance of the fact. Once this point has been grasped by society as a whole a potential source of great good can be harnessed.

In his 1995 Tory Party Conference speech the then Prime Minister, John Major, spoke of his vision of a 'wise and kindly way of life that is rooted in our history'. He was much ridiculed at the time, which is sad, because they were amongst the best words he spoke. I once took a walk from Herne Hill in South East London, through Camberwell and up to the Elephant and Castle; stopping at every pub on the way to make a note of how many charity tins each pub had. In 30 odd pubs only one had no collecting tin, and that was a noisy, loutish, lager swillery. In the Nag's Head on Camberwell New Road the locals had just had a collection for a local pensioner who had been mugged of his pension money. Further down the road at Liam Og's (a genuine Irish pub from the days before the plague of plastic Paddy pubs) the landlord puts on a pensioners' Christmas dinner in his function room with the help of the local police station. The tables are festooned with flowers, donated by a regular of his, a florist. As an image of a wise and kindly society I think that is hard to beat.

As we also live in an increasingly secular society, in which people feel ever more alienated from traditional mainstream institutions, there is a role for the pub to fill the vacuums created by an uncertain world. We can see evidence of this in rural Britain – one third of rural parishes in England and Wales have no pub – where, increasingly, communities are fighting to retain their local pubs, and even to rediscover the traditional functions of the alehouse, as pubs become post offices and village stores.

As people use pubs as surrogate means of charity collection and distribution, or as replacement local services, they are merely doing what people have done in pubs ever since the alehouse evolved into an identifiable institution as feudal society declined after the Black Death.

If only the firms that own the pubs understood the nature of the public house, they would not be having such a hard time. It is the unfavourable treatment of pubs by their owners that discourage large sections of society from patronising the pubs These tend to be the wealthiest sections of society; its opinion formers. By which I do not mean the committed family brewers but the new generation of pension fund managers, entrepreneurs, accountants and occasional spivs who have taken over some of our larger companies and pub chains, as well as the social circles they move in. Their absence from the pub divides them from the shared experience of a large bulk of the population, prevent the public house from taking a more respectable and positive role in our national life, damages the prospects of our national drink, and perverts our own perceptions of our culture.

The egalitarianism of the public house may be precisely what makes it unattractive to them. Yet it will require a general recognition by a section of society, that forswears the pub that it is, in fact, the only defining cultural institution that has any prospect of countering the alienation and fragmentation apparent in modern life.

That this is true can be seen in the way in which pubs are marketed and refurbished. The Brewers Tudor of the improved public house movement' of the 1920s and 1930s was the last attempt to define a universally coherent architectural style of public house in Britain It was necessarily retrospective, and was proximate enough to the Victorian age to react against it. Our generation cannot reinvent our town pubs, at least, as anything other than increasingly unrecognisable interpretations of the late Victorian style. For our society the Victorian imagery of the public house fulfils several important functions. The concept of 'Victorian' in itself provides security; it suggests comfort and reassurance; it underlines tacitly assumed cultural certainties. To try to redesign a post-Victorian public house is fraught with dangers. It would require pub customers to confront several issues about their perceptions of society that they would rather not address.

Modern interpretations of pubs, or trendy Yuppie pub conversions where a 'modern' style is attempted, only succeed by changing the entire nature of the beast – i.e. they cease being pubs and end up as casual restaurants, or by justifying 'modernism' in terms of foreign influences – again – produces the pub as bistro. Modernising the pub and retaining it within an identifiably British context has yet to be successfully achieved, indeed is probably not possible, while one of the functions of the pub is to provide cultural reassurance in the face of pressing uncertainties.

The pub is therefore caught on the horns of a societal dilemma. On the one hand it cannot regain its proper place as the focal point of popular British culture and society unless it reinvents itself in a modern, and relevant context, and it cannot reinvent itself because it is hidebound by the shortcomings of modern British culture in general and the specific shortcomings, of the companies who own the pub in particular.

Pub owners, with a few honourable exceptions, are loath to regard the pub as part of our national heritage which needs to be appreciated as such. They much prefer to see it as a unit of capital, from which a certain rate o return must be extracted. If a bigger rate of return can be made by bulldozing the pub and converting it into a car park then so be it. This attitude is becoming ever more prevalent as the connections between brewing and retailing become weaker.

This mentality is potentially very dangerous for the pub and for society. The pub loses any intrinsic values and becomes just another 'retail operation'. The results are clear to see, 'branded' pubs with names determined, not by local history, not by tradition, or custom, but by the transient whim of a marketing executive. Professional managers – loyal to the company bonus scheme rather than the local community – complete the picture and the pub begins to share the sanitised homogeneity of the high street. Traditional British eccentricity must be expunged for the sake of the inoffensiveness of the national brand.

It is up to the public to lay claim to a proprietary stake in their heritage, and the pub in particular. What happens when they do not is clear, look at Stonehenge. The new, revamped monarchy is already emerging as more marketable and more marketing friendly, and given the fickleness of markets the potentially dangerous consequences of this move are plain to see, but there are still publicans and drinkers who know what a pub is and what it should be. They can be found in the Nag's Head, and in Liam Og's. and visitors from all over the world – even from Perpignan and Cordoba – come and marvel at these unique places.

PUB GAMES

BY ARTHUR TAYLOR

I'm not just there for the beer, although good beer is part of it. I know I'm in the right sort of place when the first pint is tested and approved and there is time to look at the notice-board: you know the sort of thing – a flutter of bits of paper which includes the pontoon club table, darts, pool, domino and crib teams, news of social outings, raffle tickets and the like. Maybe there is something else here as well, not immediately obvious...

The simplest short-cut way to find my type of good pub is to follow the *Good Beer Guide* and look for the entries which include that ace of clubs sign which signifies 'traditional pub games played'. It isn't infallible, but at least it is a start.

I've been searching out, watching, playing and writing about pub games for forty years now – a taproom, public bar, games room odyssey of epic proportions which resulted in a book in 1976 (an introduction), another in 1992 (a progress report) and a host of articles in between. It has been relentless hard work, but there you are, someone had to do it. I expect to produce an interim study early in the millennium. I don't know how those fellows painting the Forth Bridge feel, but I'm just fine, mainly because the rewards – I mean convivial rewards, not the financial ones, are tremendous.

Consider: it is a fine sun-bright, blue-skied, breezy August Saturday in Beck Hole, North Yorkshire and I am here for the Beck Hole annual open quoits championship, first prize a bit of cash and a copper kettle. The whole of the quoits world is here, and there is knowledgeable chat about every throw – as the steel quoits 'ring' and plunge into the clay beds near the pin they are noted as 'face-gater-housekeeper', 'Q quoit', or 'Frenchman'. A very old man, seated next to one of the beds, falls out of his chair in excitement at one of the throws. From time to time we retreat to the Birch Hall Inn, just up the road, a pub which serves as general store and informal museum to the game (look at the old photographs on the wall), to try the Theakstons. In dozens of pubs in North Yorkshire and Cleveland and Tyne and Wear they play quoits.

Or: A winter evening in Swanage, in the Isle of Purbeck, Dorset. The tourists are long-gone, it is cold, wet and windy outside and at the Red Lion they have pulled out the shove halfpenny board, which is four feet long by 18 inches wide (no metrification here, thank you very much) – it is scored at the far end into square, circular and semi-circular compartments and the halfpence, English circa 1906, and Guernsey, Jersey and Irish coins of the same vintage float slowly, endlessly along the vast expanse of the board. This is very different from any sort of shove ha'penny (note the spelling) which you may have seen before. The game is 101 up and the beer is Ringwood Best Bitter and Flowers Original.

And again: The Three Horseshoes, Garsington, Oxfordshire – it is summer with heavy cloud but only intermittent showers. What appears to be the car park has suddenly been re-arranged into an arena for Oxfordshire's own skittles game: the wonderful Aunt Sally. A swan's neck swivel is inserted into a hollow post. The 'doll', the wooden target, sits on top of the swivel and players throw ash batons from a range of ten yards. The place is heaving with good-natured experts with a comment for each throw. They are drinking Draught Bass and Morrell Bitter. Just one of the local leagues in Oxfordshire has 24 divisions with ten teams in each section – this is a hugely popular game. Just look at the *Oxford Mail* on a Wednesday for the results, league tables and match commentaries. I am deeply disappointed that the Good Beer Guide casually mentions only one pub in the whole of the county which plays.

Local radio is full of people who appear to know very little about the everyday life of their region and from time to time one of them suddenly discovers the notion of pub games and there I am, spouting my stuff. 'But surely, Arthur,' they say, 'pub games have completely died out in this country.' They are astonished when I ramble on about quoits in North Yorkshire, shove halfpenny in Dorset or Aunt Sally in Oxfordshire – this is to local radio stations in North Yorkshire, Dorset and Oxfordshire respectively.

The reason for all this ignorance and confusion is, I suppose, that many of these pastimes are easily missed. They are not advertised much, if at all, and you have to be in the right place at the right time to catch them. No-one would know about quoits or Aunt Sally if they arrived at a playing pub outside playing hours or the league season; holiday-makers in Swanage would not see Isle of Purbeck shove halfpenny because the boards only come out from the back room in the off-season. The boards and the coins are delicate and not to be fooled around with.

'All right,' says the local programme presenter, invariably somewhat miffed by the secret truth and anxious to change the subject, 'what is the most popular pub game in Britain today?'

'Probably pool,' I reply. More disappointment. Surely we should not approve of pool, a commercialised, paying game, introduced from a foreign country? Pool has often displaced that old traditional English pub game, bar-billiards. Bar-billiards first appeared in Belgium in the 1920s when it was called 'Billard Russe' (why, for heaven's sake?). An English business-man, on a walking holiday on the Belgian-French border in the 1930s, saw the game and brought it to this country. It was a commercialised, paying game: 6 pence (2 $\frac{1}{2}$ p) per game, when a pint cost 4 pence (1 $\frac{1}{3}$ p). Pub games, folk games, tend to wander over frontiers and settle down without the authorities noticing until it is too late and the illegal immigrants are nicely settled in and claiming 'traditional' status.

The point about pub games is not at all that they are dying out, but they are evolving, changing all the time. The most startling development over the last twenty years, given the perpetual 'best of enemies' relationship between Britain and France, has been the enthusiastic adoption of the French boules game of pétanque. Go to Sams Hotel, in Shedfield, Hampshire (Banks Mild, Marston Bitter, Pedigree) and they will tell you the tale of customers who came back from a holiday in France in 1974, start-ed playing pétanque in the car park, gathered friends and influenced peo-ple and quickly formed the British Pétanque Association, which now con-trols the game in this country and dispatches teams to take part in the world championships every year. Scan the pages of the Good Beer Guide and you will see that pétanque is the game which is mentioned more than any other in the lists of 'traditional' pub pastimes. Please don't worry over much about that French connection – we got traditional British institutions such as crisps, chips, pigeon racing, bar-billiards, dominoes, playing cards and the National Lottery from them and the French-speaking Belgians.

I think we still maintain our tradition of eccentricity – where else but around the British pub would you find such things as conkers, clog cob-bing, conger cuddling, dwile flonking, marrow dangling, flounder stamping, worm charming, woodlice racing, toe wrestling and rhubarb thrashing? (Mind you, I've seen snail racing, sabot throwing, uphill pétanque with square boules, naked-toed log chopping, cross-country golf and potato-spearing-from-a-bicycle in France over the last year or two. And any naïve soul who thinks that French beer is undrinkable should try, for starters, Ch'Ti from the Brasserie Castelain, Angelus from the Brasserie Annoeuillin, Choulette or Sans Culotte from the Brasserie La Choulette, or Jenlain from the Brasserie Duyck).

A final visit, though, for reassurance about superior British daftness, to a Good Beer Guide recommended pub, try the Neuadd Arms Hotel at Llanwrtyd Wells in Powys (Hancocks HB, Felinfoel Double Dragon, Draught Bass, etc.). Once a year the pub organises the World Bog Snorkelling Championships, the Mountain-Bicycle Bog-Leaping Point-to-Point and the Man versus Horse versus Mountain-Bike Marathon. You don't believe me? Ring the landlord, Gordon Green, on 01591 610237 and ask for details. Now, his noticeboard is really worth reading.

A PINT OF BEER – from the malt to the glass
by Steve Sharples

From the Maltings

Malt millling

Above: The Mash Tun

Below: To the Copper

Above: Hop sacks   Below: Adding the hops

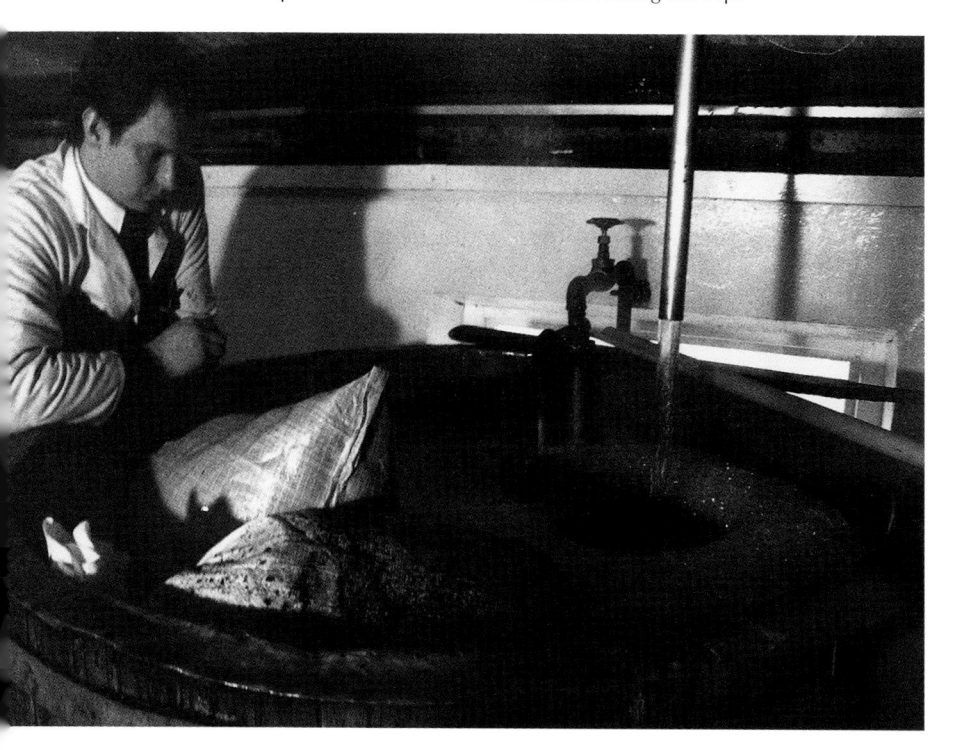

Above: The Copper

Below: The Whirlpool

Above: A vigorous fermentation   Below: Fermentation finishing

Above: Racking

Below: Ready for delivery

In the bar

Mmm…

BEER AND FOOD

BY SUSAN NOWAK

ONLY one snippet sticks in my mind from Caesar's Gallic Wars wrestled with, briefly, in the Latin as a schoolgirl. I suppose it was full of battle tactics and centurions, skirmishes with the Iceni and bra-burning Boadicea, lots of marching and road building programmes. I really can't recall. But the scene was suddenly illuminated for that bored scholar, (already sneaking into the Flask in Hampstead for an under age half of bitter), when the great commander recorded his first impressions of the 'triangular' land he had come to see and conquer. Roughly (very roughly) translated he scribbled: 'Dear Diary, the Brits are a load of louts who are into face painting and brew a strange drink from barley.' Wow! History could teach me something!

History, in fact, went on to record beer's influence on the British diet for hundreds of years to come – and, hopefully, into the new millennium. Our national beverage has never lost its charm as a drink, but somewhere along the way forfeited its place on the dining table to be relegated to the public bar. Even here it was not the natural accompaniment to food. As recently as a decade ago you could get little more than a pickled egg or bag of salted peanuts in most pubs – and then we went through a period where meals served by mine host were justly described as 'pub grub'.

But there is evidence of a happier age. An age when inns succoured the weary traveller, providing him with fine victuals accompanied, of course, by fine ale. In the early Middle Ages, Chaucer's pilgrims enjoyed veritable feasts in taverns on their way to Canterbury. A couple of hundred years later in 1512 the menu for a typical Lenten 'break fast' enjoyed by the fifth Earl of Northumberland and his lady was: 'first a loaf of bread in trenchers, two manchets, a quart of beer, a quart of wine, two pieces of salt fish, six bacconed herring, four white herring or a dish of sprats.' That should set you up for the day!

Skip another 200 years and there's Ned Smith in the London Spy writing of 'a penny worth of burnt (toasted) bread, softened in a mug of porter's guzzle'. Yuk. In the 19th century, Dickens was clearly seldom out of a pub, judging by his novels. There's Alfred Jingle's joyous anticipation of a 'Devilish good dinner – cold, but capital – peeped into the room this morning – fowls and pies and all that sort of thing' at the Blue Lion during the travels of Pickwick and co. David Copperfield lost his dinner to a barman who relieved him of the bother of eating it with the words: 'Lord bless my soul…a chop's the very think (sic) to take the head off the bad effects of that beer!' And there are many tasty pub moments in Martin Chuzzlewit. My favourite, the pleasure of Tom Pinch in a lone repast of 'well cooked steak and smoking hot potatoes' accompanied by 'a jug of most stupendous Wiltshire beer'.

Rather more recently, I snapped up The Book of Beer by Andrew Campbell in a secondhand bookshop. Written in the fifties, it gives a fascinating insight into people's dietary expectations nearly half a century ago (not to mention their sexist attitudes as evidenced in 'beer is pre-eminently a man's drink and only one out of every three women ever taste it'). His advice was to use beer to build up your lunchtime calorie count (220 a pint) alongside a ploughmans of three slices of wholemeal bread and butter (311 calories), 3 oz of cheese (400) and celery (10), totalling 940 calories midday. What you might call a calorie uncontrolled diet.

With such an historic pedigree, why has the hop failed to win the gastronomic respect it enjoys overseas? Belgium embraces a whole beer culture. In Brussels bars and restaurants beer is an honoured companion both in the glass and on the plate. Typical are mussels and bacon cooked in wheat beer, national dish carbonnade of beef braised in brown gueuze, rabbit or venison cooked in a strong, dark Trappist beer or duck with a cherry beer sauce. Bavarian breweries often have beer halls – the equivalent of the brewery tap – where robust platefuls are served with frothing tankards; an example of a brewery breakfast is veal sausages and sweet mustard with a long glass of wheat beer. In a recent visit to Austria I found their breweries and brew pubs likewise have a long tradition of marrying beer and food. I recall some of the best beer soups, game 'n' beer and serious beer dumplings I have ever tasted.

America more recently 'discovered' beer cuisine and embraced it with all the unrestrained enthusiasm they bring to anything 'new'. Let's face it, 'Sicilian peppers stuffed with anchovies, pine nuts and raisins flavoured with pale ale' is surely taking things a tad too far!

But the hop shoots of cuisine a la biere are definitely beginning to sprout here, and high time too, for the stunning and ever increasing range of beer styles in Britain just cry out to go with food and in food. A light mild or wheat beer cleanses the palate at the start of a meal, a barley wine, winter ale or Scotch 'wee heavy' are perfect after dinner tipples. Dark, dry stout is made for lobsters and oysters, a robust bitter handsome with roast beef and Yorkshire pudding, India Pale Ale powerful with smoked fish and kedgeree, a clean pilsener the partner for delicate pork escalopes – but choose a big bitter or even tongue tingling German rauchbier (smoked beer) with the roast leg and crackling. Matching beer to food is fun because there are no preconceptions. No wine waiter to sneer!

You can find some complex, vinous brews, ruby as old port, perfect with game; those beautifully balanced, fruity bitters that we Brits brew like nobody else – and must have invented, surely, to go with mature Cheddar and Stilton in a ploughmans, cold cuts of ham and beef or golden-crusted pork pie with sweet mustard pickle. Publicans, at last, are realising what a valuable ingredient they have on tap. Among the recipes they sent me for the Campaign for Real Ale's 10th anniversary *Good Pub Food Guide*, published in the summer of 1999, were enough beer dishes to make a substantial section – including pumpkin, apple and beer chutney; venison collops with cranberries and old ale; haggis and turnip fritters with real ale onion gravy, and sweet beer tart. Suddenly in the past couple of years beer has become 'sexy', popularised by an outpouring of new ales from breweries, an inpouring of unusual beers from abroad, and the opening of beer and brew restaurants from Belgo to Mash.

This rich choice encouraged me to write a recipe book entirely devoted to beer, *The Beer Cook Book*, with the full range of dishes from starters and soups through main courses including fish, meat and vegetarian, to desserts and baking. Recipes such as mash tun gammon, gigot of lamb with raspberry beer gravy, red onion tart with IPA, steak and smoked oyster pudding with oyster stout, Thomas Hardy's sticky toffee pudding and cherry beer syllabub are among them – celebrity chefs including Rick Stein, Albert Roux, Delia Smith and Keith Floyd were sufficiently turned on by beer cuisine to contribute. Originating the recipes was a great joy – and so is putting together the menu for the Guild's annual Beer Banquet; dishes made with beer, each course accompanied by beer. A recent menu opened with hop sausages, Stilton and ale twists, chestnuts glazed in Xmas ale on arrival followed by Cumbria Mature Royal ham cured in a brine containing Newcastle Brown Ale with figs steeped in Theakston Old Peculier as starter; guinea fowl cooked with Fraoch Heather Ale or, for vegetarians, asparagus, sweet pimento and Gruyere croustade with a Fraoch and honey sauce for the main course; ending with pears in porter. With coffee came chocolate beer truffles made with Schneider Aventinus. Brings a whole new meaning to Ale and Hearty!

DIVIDED THEY FALL
A history of trade associations of the brewing and pub industry

BY TIM HAMPSON

People have probably always banded together in coalitions of self interest. The family, a tribe, guilds, workers and producers, have all in their time been drawn together to defend a common cause. Butchers, bakers, even candlestick makers have all formed trade associations to fight against the actions of government or other legislators. State regulation encourages such combinations. And with every aspect of the brewing and selling of beer closely scrutinised the beer and pub industry is no exception to this. Tax, temperance, licensing law and controls on the raw materials for beer have all encouraged federations of brewers to come together.

At first there was not a single voice for the industry, or even one that spoke for the majority. In the nineteenth century brewers embraced the craft of medieval England, the brewing victualler together with those who were using the latest technology, the industrial capitalist.

Tax and control on production were the first spurs to co-operation. In the eighteenth and early nineteenth centuries Chancellors of the Exchequer would expect to fill more than a quarter of their coffers with excise from the production of beer. Until the 1760s permission was ostensibly needed before beer prices could rise, either from parliament or a Justice of the Peace. In addition the excise regulated the means of production. Malting, in particular, was rigidly controlled with revenue officers able to inspect every detail of its manufacture, including the timing and sequence of events.

Beer is a common product brewed by many, but the industry of the early nineteenth century was divided by self interest and local markets together with developing marketing and transport skills. The London brewers, who specialised in porter, were able to achieve favourable excise rates. This incensed and united country brewers who lobbied to have the tax legislation changed in 1802. But it was the introduction of the Intermediate Brewers Bill in 1822 that forced a loose coalition to take on a more formal structure. It proposed that a separate class of brewery should be created, fixing a new level of duty and price for a beer of intermediate strength which could only be sold 'off' their premises or to a specially designated category of publican.

For the economic historian this is a rich time – the contradictions between free trade and industrial efficiency, state intervention and market forces are now more clearly seen. It was also a time before issues could split people on party political lines. Though the threat of legislation encouraged brewers to seek seats in parliament, they brought with them their old loyalties as Quakers or Whigs or Tories, landowners or new industrialists. As yet there was no threat to unify them on one side. The Intermediate Brewers Bill became an Act. It flopped, but its introduction led to the setting up of the Country Brewers' Association.

In 1822, 14 members of the trade gathered together. By the end of the year there were 48, mainly comprising larger brewers in the south-east of England. The first rule of the association was: if you wanted a voice, 'cash down'. At that time the subscription was £1 per member. For 82 years the association acted on behalf of its members with its membership growing to 598. Later in the century, though the dates of formation are unclear, the London Brewers' Association and Burton Brewers' Association were formed.

In the short term the three did not act in concert and, in truth, they probably had few resources and little clout. The Beer Acts of 1830, divided brewers. The country brewers feared increased competition, while those in London, muscles hewn by aggressive free trading, saw little threat. Tradition and innovation are the dynamic, and sometimes contradictory, partners that have helped to shape the face of the modern pub industry. No more so than in the next 70 years or so, which saw pugnacious competition and an aggressive and determined scramble to acquire pubs. Few saw the need for collective activity. Indeed, probably less than 70 per cent of brewers belonged to any trade grouping.

However, four factors: tax, temperance, tumbling profits and the termination of old licences without compensation forced the industry to realise that co-operation was necessary. Brewers blamed the government for their ills. The Licensing Act of 1904 was seen as a threat to the whole industry and the pub, after years of expansion, was in decline. In 1903 the trade realised that there must be a single organisation to talk to government and the Master of the Brewers' company was asked to call a conference of the wholesale trade on 15 January 1904.

Attenders at the conference, names that still mean much to beer drinkers, Butler, Fuller, Holt, Pope, Robinson, Webster, Wells and Whitbread, to name but a few, called for 'unity of action and policy in order to strengthen the wholesale trade'. Mr T Hamilton Fox, of Fox and Sons, Farnborough, pointed out that, while there might have been reasons which kept the London and Burton brewers apart from the country brewers, he strongly believed that they were now more inclined to join in one organisation: The Brewers' Society (BS).

Limiting the effects of legislation on the brewing industry, then as now, was the main preoccupation of the Society. During the First World War prime minister and temperance campaigner, David Lloyd George, united the industry in a way that no one had ever done before. 'Drink,' he thundered, 'is doing us more damage than all the German submarines put together.' He was riding high on an anti-drink tide. Restrictions were brought in on the output and strength of beer. Consumption was limited by taxation which rose 430 per cent in the war years. And the indomitable DORA was introduced: the Defence of the Realm Act which restricted opening hours, closing pubs in the afternoon and early in the evening. It took 70 years to release the shackles of restricted opening hours on pub users.

Worse was to come with the Carlisle brewery, near a munitions factory, nationalised and the police, military, and then civil authorities given the power to close pubs if they thought their use was hindering the was effort.

Lloyd George believed Britain had three enemies, Germany, Austria and drink. Draconian controls on brewing were brought in. They could have been worse had not the Brewers' Society stood firm. By 1917 the Government realised it may have gone too far. Its prohibition colours were exposed as a summer of discontent erupted and factory workers and dockers went on strike. It was blamed on there being a shortage of alcohol and beer in particular. Restrictions were eased.

Post war, the work of the Society continued unabated with much work being done to provide evidence to the Royal Commission on Licensing which met between 1929 and 1931. Beer production had declined 50 per cent between 1919 and 1933. If the first premise of the BS was to limit the effects of legislation on the industry then the second became to promote the image of beer and pubs.

Advertising and market research were in their infancy. However, it was believed that corporate and collective advertising would benefit the brewing industry. In December 1933 the 'Beer is Best' campaign was launched. Few would have guessed that it would run in one form or another for 40 years. Beer was best for health, best for refreshment, good for fellowship, good for agriculture and good for the exchequer.

As the lights went out over Europe in 1939 at the start of the second world war, they stayed on in Britain's pubs and breweries. Winston Churchill was determined that the mistakes of the Great War were not to be made again. Pubs were the block houses on the home front and the enjoyment of beer an essential part of keeping the national morale high. The BS undertook the allocation of material to brewers as were schemes to limit output, together with the rationalisation of transport for deliveries and the supply of beer for troops overseas. The advertising space booked for the 'Beer is Best' campaign was donated to the Ministry of Information which, until the end of the war, used it for public service announcements under the 'What do I do?' banner.

In the early post-war years the society was active in opposing the Licensing Bills in parliament, including the 1948 Act, which included the state purchase of public houses in new towns (subsequently repealed) and the Society made full and detailed representations to the Home Office prior to the Licensing Bill of 1961.

The industry's case to the Monopolies Commission in 1966 was undertaken by the BS. Indeed, since 1966, the industry has been subject to at least 32 investigations and interventions by the government and the European Union. This does not include inquiries into, or legislation on, health related or environmental issues, trading standards, law and order matters or licensing law.

As legislators at local and national level have become more sophisticated so the brewing and pub industry trade association has had to adapt. The accession of the UK to the EEC added another dimension to the Society's operations and the Society joined the EFTA brewers' organisation and subsequently the Communaute de Travail Brasseurs du Marche Commun (CBMC).

In 1989, following an investigation by the Monopolies and Mergers Commission, the Beer Orders were published. National companies were forced to sell or let free of the tie 50 per cent of their pubs above 2,000, and their tenants were able to buy cask conditioned guest beer from a source of their choice. At a stroke legislators changed the structure of national companies and forced smaller companies to rethink business strategies.

As a result the focus of the industry's trade association had to change, as did the name. In 1994 the Brewers' Society became the Brewers and Licensed Retailers Association (BLRA). The change of name signified the realignment in the industry. Some companies had ceased to brew and were only retailers and some sold their pubs and became just brewers. In addition, many newly formed, non-brewing, pub-owning companies who wanted to have the representation of a trade association were applying for membership of the BLRA.

As in 1822 and 1904 the change in name reflected the realities of the time. Since the fledgling Country Brewers' Association there has been an intimate relationship between politics and the business of the brewing and pub industry that underlines the need for an effective industry trade association. Licensing law, the excessive tax on beer, the promotion of the image of beer and pubs, and temperance are not issues that will go away and the BLRA (or its Successor) will be there on the front line.

Chronology

1822 – Country Brewers' Society established

Sometime between 1822 and 1904 the London Brewers' Association and the Burton Brewers' Association were established. Exact dates unknown.

1904 – Brewers' Society formed, being a federation of the Country Brewers' Society, the London Brewers' Association and the Burton Brewers' Association.

1994 – Following structural changes in the industry the Brewers' Society changes its name to the Brewers' and Licensed Retailers' Association. Membership Includes brewers owning pubs, larger pub operators and brewers.

1995 – Articles of association changed to allow international brewers not brewing in the UK to become associate members.

MESSAGE IN A BOTTLE

BY RICHARD MORRICE

There's something rather solid and nice about a bottle of beer. It has presence and solidity. If the brewer has done his job properly the bottle labels won't just tell you the strength and quantity of the contents but they'll tell you a little bit about the brewery or the beer type or its heritage.

Over the years we have been rather fond of our bottled beers. They have been produced to commemorate great events such as VE Day and the Coronation. Not surprisingly there is a fascinating bottled beer museum at Tolly Cobbold in Ipswich with examples of different beers which go back to the time of the Napoleonic Wars. Classic bottled beers such as Thomas Hardy from Eldridge Pope are 'laid down' by beer aficionados for up to 25 years and enjoyed by groups of admiring imbibers.

My first experience of beer was the dark and then, delicious Forest Brown from Whitbread which I bought in one pint London brewer bottles from an off-licence near to where I lived. The choice in the shop was very limited; brown and light ales were the order of the day and the product was always handed to you over the counter in a somewhat severe-looking brown paper bag.

Given this, it is not surprising that in the late '70s it looked as though bottled beers were going to disappear from the British scene altogether. All the interest went out of them. Beers that were supplied in bottles to the pubs and clubs were in the main a dull commodity and no-one seemed to care about them. Brewers boasted that they would make a standard London half pint or pint returnable bottle last for in excess of forty trips before it finally collapsed in a heap of glass dust. The product was shabby with cheap, dull labels stuck haphazardly onto scuffed, chipped bottles.

Big breweries like John Smith's shut down their bottling lines altogether and sent beers away to sub-contractors. They cancelled the minuscule amount of development work and investment which they had been applying to the bottled beer sector.

And then, there were faint signs of the renaissance in bottled beers. Regional brewers of quality and repute such as Shepherd Neame at Faversham in Kent realised that the only sensible option that they had for increasing their distribution, outside their core trading areas was bottled beer.

Cans were associated with cheap and commodity products and traditional ale producers felt (rightly or wrongly) that they tainted the beer and the cost of cask beer and the associated beer engines for use in the pubs made large-scale expansion in this area cost prohibitive for many brewers.

Some ten years ago or more Shepherd Neame produced a beautifully crafted set of beers – Spitfire, Bishop's Finger and others. They presented them with some trepidation to the supermarkets who had seen nothing quite like them before and there was cautious optimism that the brands might sell a case or two a week in some of the larger stores.

To meet the requirements of the buyers the bottles were packed into small cases (after all, there wasn't going to be a huge demand was there?). The caution was soon thrown to the winds, the early stocks were cleared off the shelves within days of arriving and it was clear that a new market was born.

Since then the companies which got into the market early and have worked hard, Morland's, Shepherd Neame, Marston's and others, have maintained their place and developed ranges of interesting beers.

Most large supermarkets now have between 80 and 90 premium bottled ales available to their customers and the total market is worth over 50 million pounds a year.

New entrants join the swelling ranks on a weekly basis.

And that's just the supermarkets and off licences.

Young people love to drink premium lagers in bottles in pubs and clubs. Old fuddy duddys like me may complain about the prices paid but brands like Becks and Holsten in bottles outsell their draught counterparts many times over.

Having been on the critical list twenty-five years ago the bottled beer market is now in rude good health. It accounts for over ten percent of the total UK beer market and figures are rising year by year. As with all these things there are, of course, dangers ahead – the brewers must keep the interest alive by bringing in new products and they must ensure that the beers are presented in top condition and represent good value for money.

Bottled beers represent the chance for drinkers to sample all types of different brews at a price they can afford. They give the industry a chance to send all beer drinkers a message in a bottle.

BEER IS BEST
The collective advertising of beer

BY FIONA WOOD

The idea of a generic advertising campaign for British beer was first suggested in 1929 but several brewing companies with national status had already began to use advertising and methods of market analysis to improve brand loyalty. Individual companies such as Guinness, Bass and Whitbread had already embarked on national marketing schemes from the late nineteenth century, but the full force of national advertising campaigns did not become apparent until the early 1900s. In 1928 Guinness launched, with the assistance of the leading London advertising agency SH Benson, its first national campaign with the slogan 'Guinness Is Good For You'. By 1933 Guinness was by far the largest spender on advertising with Bass and the slogan, 'Great Stuff This Bass'; Watneys with 'What We Want Is Watney's' and Whitbread in hot pursuit. The smaller companies which looked to more local markets also dabbled with advertising such as George's Bristol brewery, but overall the amount of expenditure was modest in relation to sales.

During the inter-war years beer consumption had fallen sharply due to the depression and high unemployment, accompanied by high beer duties, causing widespread alarm in the trade and the Brewers' Society. In 1933 duty was reduced on the understanding that brewers would increase the gravity of their beers and reduce the price by ld. In consideration of the reduction in duty the trade was pledged to do its utmost to increase output in order to counteract loss of revenue by the exchequer and to arrest the depressed state of agriculture by the absorption of more home-grown barley. Later that year the Brewers' Society appointed the London Press Exchange as advertising agents to supervise the creative work. Little did the brewers realise that the campaign would turn out to be one of the largest co-operative ventures of its day and that it was to last for almost forty years.

Initially the campaign was financed by a levy supported by 85 per cent of society members. Within a year the support was almost 100 per cent. The launch date was set for 1st December, 1933 and, ironically, coincided with the week in which prohibition ended in the United States. Formulation of plans for the campaign however did not escape the attentive eye of the UK Temperance Alliance who immediately sought to counteract the campaign and announced: 'Brewers Plans Revealed: Sinister Campaign to Enslave Youth to the Drink Habit.' In fighting form the brewer's launched their slogan which was a simple but powerful strapline, 'Beer is Best', which immediately captured the attention of the British public. The campaign rationale had wide appeal placing emphasis on the wholesomeness of ingredients, the relationship between beer and recreation. and the role of the public house as a social centre. Beer was best for health, best for refreshment, for good fellowship, good for agriculture and good for the Exchequer. The temperance interest responded with: 'Beer is Best Left Alone', but this had little impact. On the contrary a flurry of simple punchy slogans followed which were effectively interpreted into powerful colourful imagery based on commissioned designs by 'Rix' and Royal Academy artist Keith Henderson. At least 62 different images were used in 1935 and 26 in 1936. The slogans ran 'For Bodily Health Beer is Best', 'To Set a Man up For Winter – Beer is Best', 'For an A1 People – Beer is Best', posters of which are reproduced today by the Brewers and Licensed Retailers Association successor to the Brewers' Society.

The most effective method of advertising, in addition to drip mats, dart boards, trays, calendars, even motor lorry radiators, was in the form of huge posters on roadside hoardings. The first campaign in September, 1934 featured 8,500 roadside posters declaring 'Here's to the Barley Crop', combined with press adverts in newspapers totalling a circulation of 92 million. By 1937 the pace of creative output was taking its toll and a new agency, Crawfords, was brought into the campaign. A cartoon figure – Mr XXX was introduced to 'Xplain' the facts about beer, but was soon supplanted by the single simple slogan – 'Stick to Beer'. By 1939, regular press adverts were appearing in around 90 daily and Sunday newspapers and some 500 weeklies. During the first five years of the campaign up to 1938 it has been estimated to have cost the brewers £139,000 per year, approximately £6.5 million at today's prices. In terms of impact on consumption beer sales said it all and recovered from an all time low of 17.9 million barrels in 1933 to 24.6 million by 1939.

A turn of events came again with the onset of the second world war and the threat of invasion and defeat both very real. The Brewers' Society rallied support for the war effort by giving all its newspaper space to the Ministry of Information which used it for public service announcements under the 'What Do I Do…?' banner until the end of 1945. Messages to the public ranged from simple domestic issues, such as saving coal and gas or canning beans, to full military instructions on how to cope with an airborne invasion. In effect the brewers had managed to maintain public interest in their product by the patriotism and spirit of their advertising. After the War the demands on brewers were even greater. Post-war restrictions on buildings and raw materials meant that the brewers had difficulty supplying demand for beer and few pubs could be refurbished until after the impact of war damage had been assessed.

The campaign continued to toe the patriotic line supporting the country's drive for exports in the form of 'After a Good Day's Work for Britain, that's when beer is best'. After the war, particularly in view of the excess of demand over supply, the direct advertising of beer was suspended. In its place the society turned its attention to publicising the public house as a social centre and its place in the life of the community. Initially this was conveyed by the 'At The Friendly Inn…' series which was introduced in 1948 by another new agency, Pritchard Wood and Partners, who tied the series in with the general 'drive for exports' promoted by the government. This was later accompanied by 'advertorials' which sought to explain the role of the brewer, the landlord, the cellarman, the inn sign, and the role of the Chancellor of the Exchequer. The result was a series of prestige adverts under the banner 'Welcome To The Inns of Britain' to coincide with the Festival of Britain in 1951.

It is clear that during the war the public house re-established its central place in British leisure activity, but this was primarily a situation caused by lack of alternatives rather than positive preferences. The vestiges of wartime restrictions had meant that essential repairs and maintenance of the brewers' tied estates had been postponed which, together with increasing competition from alternative forms of leisure such as coffee bars, television and teenage culture, presented the brewers with an enormous challenge into the 1950s. The impact on the level of sales was severe. By 1959 the beer market had declined to 23.7 million barrels which was only marginally higher than the depression years of 1936 and 1937. The brewers reacted with the appointment of a new agency, SH Benson again, who launched a two-pronged attack promoting both pubs and beer and expressed in the slogans 'Let's Have One At The Local' in 1953 and a year later switched emphasis to 'Good Wholesome Beer' which was produced in the form of a song.

In 1956 a new three phase poster campaign began. The first stage had a basis of at least 20 of the most striking and powerful designs to be created since the launch of 'Beer is Best' in 1933. The tag line was 'Beer – The Best Long Drink In The World' which again made the link between beer and its health promoting qualities expressed in the form of sports and outdoor pursuits employing cartoonists such as Thelwell to add humour. By 1959, during the year of a General Election, the brewers caught the attention of the voting public by inverting the watchword to 'Which is the best long drink in the world?' and turned the whole campaign into an election issue. The great 'beer election' asked the pub-going public to express their preference for draught or bottled by using the ballot box. There were posters, campaign songs and authentic voting slips along with ballot boxes in pubs. The 'beer election' resulted in a draw, but in terms of market research the brewers realised that it told them a lot more about the changing nature of the beer market when the share of bottled beers was much larger than today.

With the turn of another decade came further challenges from alternative leisure pursuits and the emphasis turned away from beer to the twin themes of beer and pubs. The message for beer was kept simple with 'Beer – it's Lovely' while the Brewers' Society concentrated its efforts in terms of both finance and creative dynamism into the advertising of pubs. A whole gamut of slogans was produced which clearly reflected the increasing complexity of the emerging beer market. Emphasis was placed upon the uniqueness and conviviality of the great British pub. Slogans included 'Pubs and the People', 'I Like Pubs', 'Let's all Meet at the Pub', 'Meet Me Under the Clock' (in the pub) and – noting the rapid growth in the number of licensed clubs – 'Make The Pub Your Club'.

The inevitable grip of television on an increasingly discerning population could not be ignored and in 1964 the brewers launched their first national television advertising campaign using a series of commercials called 'Look in At the Local', which ran for more than three years. Each commercial featured a well-known personality of the day dropping in at their local: footballers Dennis Law and Bobby Moore; cricketers Tom

Graveney and Fred Trueman; boxer Billy Walker; author Monica Dickens, thriller writer Leslie Charteris and The Archers writer Edward J Mason. Press adverts backed up the theme using the stars of the television advertisements and others such as Dora Bryan and Boris Karloff.

By the end of the Sixties the power of generic advertising began to dwindle as the choice of beers and variety of pubs grew. Targeting the general consumer became more difficult as more people were using pubs, in particular women, and consumers became more discerning, which was expressed by the growing complexity of the beer market. To complicate the situation further a Government inquiry into the industry resulted in the issue of a Monopolies Commission Report in 1969. In 1970 there was a final burst of television advertising with the appointment of a new agency Doyle Dane Bembach and the notion of the 'Packaged Pint' was launched. The commercial – 'For the Price of a Pint' – emphasised to the public the added value of the pub and the services and amenities which are included in the price of a pint of beer. The commercial utilised an unique animation technique drawn by cartoonist Bill Tidy and although impressively received by the public the contract with Doyle Dane Bembach failed to be renewed. By 1971 it was clear to members of the Society that collective advertising had lost its force. The Society turned its attention to public relations, giving its publicity committee that name in April 1971, at which point collective advertising ceased.

GENTLE GIANTS
The dray horses

BY ROY BAILEY

'Giants were on the earth in those days', states the bible, and some of them are with us still. Not the men that *Genesis* refers to, but horses.

There are seven major English breweries who still use dray horses for delivering beer – Wadworth, Youngs, Thwaites, Samuel Smith, Adnams, Hook Norton and Tetleys – and several more, such as Fullers, Whitbread, Courage and Robinsons, who maintain teams just for ceremonial occasions and shows. Others, such as Greene King, Ringwood and even a new micro such as the Cottage Brewery of Somerset, hire in horses to pull their promotional drays. The horses used by these companies are a far cry from the highly-strung and pampered creatures on which so many hopeful enthusiasts invest large sums of money in bookies' shops, and which aristocratic ladies urge over fences at Badminton and Hickstead.

Unlike these light, slim-legged racehorses and hunters, which are descended from three Arab stallions brought over to England in the seventeenthth century, dray horses are the descendants of the Great Horse which used to roam the plains of Europe and which was introduced into England by William the Conqueror as a battle steed. Although probably resembling a short-legged Suffolk Punch rather than a Shire, they were much larger than the native ponies, and may have contributed as much as the archers to the defeat of the Saxons at Hastings.

From then until the introduction of gunpowder, these massive beasts, known as 'destriers' and carrying a weight of man and armour of up to 400 lbs, were almost invincible. Once heavy armour had become obsolete and horsemen wore leather rather than plate steel, the demand was for lighter, more manoeuvrable steeds. In the seventeenth century, Cromwell imported horses from 'Barbarie', and crossed them with the native stock to produce a mount suitable for his all-conquering Ironsides in the Civil War.

No longer an instrument of war, the heavy horse found its way into agriculture and commerce, and gradually superseded the ox for haulage work. The intensification of farming after the enclosures, the spread of the canal network, and the rise of the big common brewers in the eighteenth century, with their need to transport casks of beer over long distances, created a demand for powerful horses.

By the end of the nineteenth century a number of distinct breeds had come into existence, each with its own society. Today Percherons, Suffolk Punches, Clydesdales and Ardennes are popular breeds, but the best known is the Shire, normally black or dark brown with a white face and feathers (long hair around the hoofs). Some superb specimens of this breed, which can stand anything up to 19 hands (6ft. 4in.) at the shoulder and weigh nearly a ton, are on display to the public at the Courage Shire Horse Centre at Maidenhead Thicket in Berkshire, and Youngs maintain a large working stable of ten Shires, two Percherons and two Suffolks at their brewery in Wandsworth. In 1998 their horses took over the drawing of the Lord Mayor of London's coach from Whitbread.

Adnams, rather surprisingly, also use Percherons rather than the distinctive chestnut Suffolks for deliveries around the quiet seaside town of Southwold. Sam Smiths and Tetleys, as you would expect from individualistic Yorkshiremen, use grey Shires, while their neighbours Thwaites, across the Pennines in Lancashire, have four splendid jet black Shires.

1999 marked the 25th anniversary of Wadworths' re-introduction of these large and gentle beasts for local deliveries around Devizes; a move that was made for economic reasons in the '70s when there was an oil crisis and which is still valid. As with real ale, Youngs never lost faith in their horses, although it must have been a great temptation in the 1920s, when everyone was changing over to motor transport. Vaux, the former Sunderland brewers, who had 120 horses in 1911, reduced their stable at this time to just three beasts, which were used merely to move broken glass around the brewery, and most breweries did away with horse transport completely.

Heavy horse numbers had already been depleted during World War I, when many brewery teams were conscripted to haul guns in the mud of Flanders, but it was estimated that there were 2 million working heavy horses in Britain in the immediate post-war years. Natural wastage and the slaughtering of more than 200,000 after World War II meant that by 1950 the heavy horse was practically extinct, with less than 2,000 remaining. They found a champion in Sir Winston Churchill, who wrote, 'I have always considered that the substitution of the Internal Combustion Engine for the horse marked a very gloomy passage in the progress of mankind'.

Thankfully, the pendulum swung back. Not only the increasing cost and scarcity of oil, but the 'green' revolution in the '60s persuaded a number of breweries to re-introduce dray horses for local deliveries. From the purely financial aspect, Youngs point out that a four-year-old Shire horse costs about £2,000 a year to run as opposed to £50,000 for a lorry, it has an effective working life of 10 to15 years, doesn't depreciate in value or require new tyres, and when a horse-drawn dray is stuck in a traffic jam, its engine is not burning expensive fuel. The exhaust products are rather better for the roses, too!

Being considerably more intelligent creatures than an HGV, dray horses soon learn their route and the location of the various licensed premises; a characteristic which can be useful. When a Young's dray was rammed from behind by a car in Wandsworth High Street one day, the startled horses reared up, threw off the driver and his mate, and set off down the road. But they didn't bolt; they merely ran on to the next pub on the round!

Naturally, the work of dray horses inclines them towards the appreciation of their employers' products. The normal diet for a working horse is bran, 'chop' (chopped hay), sugar beet and black treacle fed five or six times a day, but they all enjoy their occasional treat of a pint or two of ale. And not just ale, in some cases.

Thunderer was captured from the Russians at the siege of Sevastopol by Captain Aloysius Ward of the Sheffield brewing family and, because of his great strength, was used by the company to deliver the heavier loads around the hilly suburbs of the city. His favourite tipple was, naturally, vodka, of which he expected a gill at every pub he visited on delivery day. Alas, such indulgence brought the inevitable result. Thunderer collapsed on Snig Hill in the winter of 1859, and although revived by a half bottle of vodka, he died after staggering a few hundred yards. Obviously, even in the equine world, beer is best.

Contrary to popular opinion, oats are not a staple part of a dray horse's diet – in fact, they are bad for heavy horses. They can make the blood too rich and cause colic, and are therefore only fed in small quantities when the animals are working. Nevertheless, the fallacy explains the amusing story told by John Young about the time when his head brewer ordered some expensive flaked oats for a batch of Oatmeal Stout. When they failed to arrive in the brewhouse, he rang the supplier and was told that the oats had been delivered several days earlier. Enquiries revealed that the security guard at the gate had sent the consignment around to the stables!

In an age of increasing environmental awareness and a desire by many people to re-capture the best of the past, the public relations benefits of dray horses are as important as the financial ones, which is why breweries display their teams at agricultural and other shows, and engage in charity work. Traditional ale and a traditional form of transport go well together in the public mind, like mild and bitter. The sight of a brewery team plodding sedately past with a consignment of ale induces a feeling of nostalgic well-being in all but the most churlish, as events in December 1971 demonstrated.

In that month, Leeds Corporation Planning and Traffic Management Committee suggested to Tetleys that the brewery co-operate in limiting its horse-drawn deliveries because the drays were holding up traffic in the city centre. In what they described as 'the charge of the write brigade', the Yorkshire Evening Post was inundated with thousands of letters – every single one supporting the horses. One lady wrote, 'These beautiful animals with their gentle strength are a precious part of our heritage and surely should be permitted to give some pleasure and colour to our ever more drab, dreary and even poisoned environment.' Not all the letters were that polite, and after four days the Corporation backed down.

Most brewers' drays, like the two owned by Wadworth, are purpose built and can be up to a century old, lovingly restored and maintained, with 16 coats of paint and two of lacquer, and beautifully embellished. The ones used on the public roads for deliveries tend to be flatbeds with modern wheels and rubber tyres, but the show drays often resemble the deep old hay wains made famous by John Constable, and have the genuine old multi-spoked wooden wheels with iron rims. The polished black leather harness with burnished brass and steel fittings that the horses wear is also very traditional, and they are often resplendent with brightly-coloured ribbons and bows on their plaited manes and tails.

If brewery workers are a special breed, then the horsemen are extra special. Whether they have come from other brewery work, as is the case with Gordon Snook and his three colleagues at Wadworths, or have spent a lifetime with horses, like Charles Beardmore and David Clarkson at Thwaites, they are patient, gentle men who love their big charges, and are happy to spend long hours caring for them.

So when you next see a team of elaborately-harnessed draught horses pulling an example of the wainwright's and wheelwright's art laden with that of the cooper and brewer, remember that you are looking at a collection of the country's finest traditional crafts – a living, working piece of an England that very nearly vanished without trace.

AND FINALLY...

BY BARRIE PEPPER

Since its formation in 1989 the Guild has moved from strength to strength. Its reputation has never been higher; its influence continues to grow and many organisations in the beer and pub world respect it and seek the views of its members on all manner of subjects. Its membership spreads across the world and through many professions. The original objects of improving standards and our status and giving the public a greater understanding of beer and brewing have been met in so many ways. This book is probably the most obvious way of defining our purpose, the ways we set about achieving it and the consequent results be they lasting and manifest or ephemeral and thought provoking.

It has been my duty and great pleasure to act as Chairman of the Guild in its growth years. Michael Jackson saw it through the teething period and Susan Nowak has been able to take it forward with a strong membership base, a firm financial structure and a sound international integrity. There are, of course, many others in the Guild who should be mentioned for their hard work and effort but in making such a list it is so easy to leave someone out. But they know who they are and so do I.

Our work in the first decade included organising some impressive seminars on such disparate topics as Pale Ale, Louis Pasteur and Hops. Our visits have taken us to Belgium, Holland, France, Germany, Austria and the Czech Republic and to breweries large and small the length and breadth of Britain, to hop merchants and maltsters, and sundry other places connected with the brewing and pub industry. We even visited a distillery for as

Michael Jackson said at the time: 'What is whisky? Merely beer taken a stage further!'

Beer has never been given the opportunity to shine like wine. Until now that is. Newspapers and magazines have accepted it as standard that they should have a wine column but only in the last few years has the job of beer writer become part of the journalistic establishment. Even now recent research commissioned by CAMRA and Whitbread showed that despite the fact that here in Britain, while we drink three times as much beer as wine, wine gets four times as much press coverage as beer.

You can help to redress this lack of balance. You have already done so by buying or borrowing this book. Now it is your turn to spread the word and the next time you see this, or indeed any book on beer and pubs, hovering around in the section often marked as 'Food and Wine' in a book shop, then move it to a more advantageous position. And then go and drink a beer.

Cheers!

Barrie Pepper
Leeds, June 2000

INDEX

BY DAVE HALL

All entries in **bold** type refer to Breweries, both extant and extinct.
Entries in *italic* type refer to individual beers.

Adnams, Southwold	149
Allied Breweries	21, 41
Alloa Brewery, Alloa	51
Allsopp, Samuel	19, 20
Allsopp's, Burton on Trent	41
Aunt Sally	128
Bacterium Club (Institute of Brewing)	20
bar billiards	129
Barclay Perkins, London	15
Barnsley Brewery Co.	31
Bass	4,19, 20, 21,30, 90-3
Bateman's XB	83
Batham's Best Bitter	83
Beamish & Crawford, Cork	57
Beer Writers, British Guild of	xiii, 153
Belhaven, Dunbar	51
Belloc, Hilaire	118
Biddy Early Brewery, Inagh	58
Boddington's Brewery, Manchester	20, 61, 63
Borrow, George	118
Borve Brewery, nr Aberdeen	52
Braime's Tadcaster Breweries	29
Brain's, Cardiff	48, 49
Brain's Bitter	83
Brakspear's Bitter	83

Brewers and Licensed Retailers Association	139
Brewers Company	14
Brewers' Society	137-9, 144-7
British Guild of Beer Writers	xiii, 153
Broughton Brewery, Broughton	53
Buckley's, Llanelli	48
Bullmastiff Brewery, Cardiff	48, 49
Burton (up)on Trent	9, 15, 17-22
Burton Bridge Brewery, Burton	21
Burton Union, system of fermentation	20
Caffrey, Thomas R	58
Caledonian Brewery, Edinburgh	51
Calvert's Anchor Brewery, London	15
Campbell, Archibald	24
CAMRA (Campaign for Real Ale)	94-8
Carlsberg, Copenhagen	87-8
Carlsberg Tetley	21
Cattle's Brewery, Pocklington	30
Charrington	20
Courage	15, 31
Dickens, Charles	115-7
Drybrough, Andrew	24
Durden Park Beer Circle	11

INDEX

Edinburgh	23-6	Maclay's, Alloa	51
entire butt ale	32, 33-4	Manchester	60-4
Everards, Leicester	20	**Mann, Crossman & Paulin**, Burton	20
		Marston, J	19
Felinfoel Brewery, Llanelli	49	**Marston, Thompson & Evershed**,	
Fullers, Chiswick	16	Burton	21
Fuller's ESB	83	*Pedigree Bitter*	21
		McEwan, Wm., & Co, Edinburgh	24, 25
Gale's Prize Old Ale	83	*McMullen's Original AK*	83
Guinness	3, 4, 9, 34, 54, 55-6, 143	**McQuat Brewery**, Leeds	30
Guinness Foreign Extra Stout	33	**Meux and Co**, London	15
		Milne AA	115
Hammond's Brewery, Bradford	30	Monopolies Commission	138
Hancock's Brewery, Cardiff	49	**Murphy**, Cork	57
Hansen, Emil Christian	2, 3		
Harviestoun Brewery, Dollar	52	**New Brewery**, Tadcaster	29
Harwood, Ralph	14, 32, 33-4		
Hilden Brewery, Lisburn	58	**Orkney Brewery**	52
Hinde's Brewery, Darlington	30	Orwell, George	119-20
Hoare and Co, London	15		
Hodgson, George	9, 19, 101-2	pale ale	8
Holt's Brewery, Manchester	61, 62	*Palmer's Best Bitter*	84
Holt's Bitter	83	Pasteur, Louis	2, 3, 85-9
Hotham and Company		*Pedigree Bitter*	21
see Tadcaster Tower Brewery		Pepys, Samuel	117
Hyde's Brewery, Manchester	61, 62	pétanque	129
		Plassey Brewery, nr. Wrexham	49
Ind Coope	20, 21	porter	8-9, 14-6, 32-5, 68
Independent Family Brewers		**Porterhouse Brewery**, Dublin	58
of Britain	81-2		
India Pale Ale	9, 19, 24, 67-8, 102	quoits	127-8
Institute of Brewing	20		
		Reid and Co, London	15
Jennings Bitter	83	Reinheitsgebot	41
Jerome, Jerome K	117-8	**Robinson's Brewery**, Stockport	61-2
John Smith, Tadcaster	28, 29, 31	*Robinson's Old Stockport Bitter*	84
Johnson, Samuel	119	**Rochdale and Manor Brewery**	30
		Rodenbach, Belgium	33
Keats, John	118-9		
		Samuel Smith,	
lager	3, 5, 21, 40-4	Tadcaster	27-8, 29-30, 149
Leeds City Breweries	29	Scottish & Newcastle	51
Lees Brewery, Manchester	61	Scottish Courage	23, 31
London, Jack	120	Shakespeare, William	117
Lorimer & Clark, Edinburgh	51	**Shepherd Neame**, Faversham	36-9, 141
		Spitfire Premium Bitter	38-9

INDEX

shove halfpenny	128	**Truman**, London	8, 20
small beer	2		
Smith, John, Tadcaster	28,29, 31	**Victoria Brewery**, Burton Salmon	30
Smith, Samuel, Tadcaster	27-8, 29-30, 149	**Victoria Brewery**, Tadcaster	29
Smithwick's, Kilkenny	56-7	**Wadworths**, Devizes	149, 151
Southwark, London	13-6	Walkers	20
Spitfire Premium Bitter	38-9	**Watneys Stag Brewery**, London	16
		Whitbread	15, 16, 34, 63, 86, 89
table beer	2, 7	**Whitewater Brewery**, Kilkeel	58
Tadcaster Tower Brewery	28-9, 30	**Whitworth Brewery**, Wath upon Dearne	31
Tadcaster	27-31		
Taylor's Landlord	84	Wodehouse, PG	120
Tennents, Glasgow	41, 50, 52	Wolverhampton & Dudley Breweries	21
Tetleys, Leeds	149, 151	**Wrexham Lager Company**	41, 49
Thackeray, William Makepeace	119	Wrexham	46
Thomas, Dylan	120		
Thompson, J	19	**Yates Brewery**, Manchester	31
Thwaites, Blackburn	149, 152	Younger, William	24
Thwaites Bitter	84	**Younger, Wm., & Co**, Edinburgh	11, 24
Tomintoul Brewery, Highlands	52	**Young's**, Wandsworth	16, 149, 150
Tomos Watkin Brewery, Llandeilo	49	*Young's Bitter*	84

BEER GLORIOUS BEER